Fight for Rights in Modern Britain

Depth Study

SERIES EDITOR
Aaron Wilkes

Lindsay Bruce   **Rebecca Carter**
Alex Fairlamb   **Teni Gogo**   **Dan Lyndon-Cohen**
Josh Preye Garry   **Aaron Wilkes**

OXFORD
UNIVERSITY PRESS

OXFORD UNIVERSITY PRESS

Great Clarendon Street, Oxford, OX2 6DP, United Kingdom

Oxford University Press is a department of the University of Oxford. It furthers the University's objective of excellence in research, scholarship, and education by publishing worldwide. Oxford is a registered trade mark of Oxford University Press in the UK and in certain other countries.

First published in 2023

British Library Cataloguing in Publication Data
Data available

978-1-382-04239-0

978-1-382-04237-6 (ebook)

978-1-382-04238-3 (Kerboodle Digital Book)

10 9 8 7 6 5 4 3 2 1

MIX
Paper | Supporting responsible forestry
FSC www.fsc.org FSC® C007785

The manufacturing process conforms to the environmental regulations of the country of origin.

Printed in the United Kingdom by Bell & Bain

Acknowledgements

The publisher and authors would like to thank the following for permission to use photographs and other copyright material:

Lesley Abdela: 'The impact of legislation on women's lives', talking to the British Library in 2013. Reproduced by permission of the British Library; **Diane Atkinson:** *The Suffragettes: In Pictures* published in 2010 by The History Press. Reproduced by permission of The History Press; **Paul Baker:** *Outrageous! The Story of Section 28 and Britain's Battle for LGBT Education*, published by Reaktion Books. Reproduced by permission of the publisher; **Lisa Berry-Waite:** 'Obtaining state aid for the blind: The 1920 Blind March', The National Archives, 16 August 2022. Reproduced under the Open Government Licence v3.0; **Bikini Kill:** 'Double Dare Ya', track by Bikini Kill, 1991. Reproduced by permission of the Buck Music Group; **Giti Chandra** and **Irma Erlingsdóttir:** *The Routledge Handbook of the Politics of the #MeToo Movement*, published by Routledge, 2020. Reproduced by permission of the Publisher; **Mollie Clarke:** 'HIV/AIDS and the LGBTQ+ community: Education, care and support', The National Archives, 1 March 2021. Reproduced under the Open Government Licence v3.0; **Rhian Daly:** 'Nine things you need to know about returning riot grrrl game-changers Bikini Kill' published by NME, 16 Jan 2019. © NME Networks. Reproduced by permission of NME Networks; **Disability Nottinghamshire:** 'Social Model vs Medical Model of disability', published by Disability Nottinghamshire. Reproduced by permission of the publisher; **John Evans:** 'The Independent Living Movement in the UK', © Independent Living Institute. Reproduced by permission of Independent Living Institute; **Zoe Fairbairns:** 'Marriage and civil partnership', talking to the British Library in March 2013. Reproduced by permission of the British Library; **Chris Godfrey:** 'Section 28 protesters 30 years on: 'We were arrested and put in a cell up by Big Ben'', The Guardian, 27 March 2018. Copyright Guardian News & Media Ltd 2023. Reproduced by permission of Guardian News & Media Ltd; **Eddy Grant:** 'Electric Avenue', song by Eddy Grant. Reproduced by permission from Sony Music Publishing; **Katherine A. Hubbard:** 'Lesbian Community and Activism in Britain 1940s–1970s: An Interview with Cynthia Reid'. Reproduced under Creative Commons CC BY license; **Vicky Iglikowski-Broad:** 'Fifty years since the 1970 Equal Pay Act', The National Archives, 29 May 2020. Reproduced under the Open Government Licence v3.0; **Kim Knott:** 'Moving People Changing Places: South Asians Making Britain', © Kim Knott, 2011. Reproduced with permission from Sundari Anitha and Ruth Pearson; **Barbara Lisicki:** 'Block Telethon 1992 – the day we pissed on pity', 16 February 2018. Courtesy of National Disability Arts Collection and Archive (www.the-ndaca.org); **Nishah Malik:** 'From The Archive: Women's Liberation, Miniskirts and The Pill in 60s and 70s Britain', British Online Archives, 1 February 2022. Reproduced by permission of the British Online Archives; **Caitlin Moran:** 'How much has life really changed for women since the Nineties?' published by Stylist. Reproduced by permission of Stylist; **Jasmine Pierre:** 'From Brixton 1981 to BLM: reflections on Black uprisings' published by Museum of London, 21 March 2022. Reproduced by permission of Museum of London; **Fern Riddell:** 'Suffragettes, violence and militancy', published by British Library, 6 Feb 2018. Reproduced by permission of the British Library; **Dr Fern Riddell** and **Professor Krista Cowman:** 'Suffrage 100 – Did militancy help or hinder the fight for the franchise?' recorded on 20 February 2018 at the National Archives. Reproduced under the Open Government License v3.0; **Damon Rose:** 'Formerly known as the Spastics Society: The importance of charity names', published by BBC News. Reproduced with permission of BBC News at bbc.co.uk/news; **Polly Russell** and **Margaretta Jolly (eds.):** *Unfinished Business: The Fight for Women's Rights*, published by British Library Publishing, 2020. Reproduced by permission of the Publisher; **Mel Sherwood:** 'Sisters in arms: the Women's Liberation Movement', BBC History Extra, 9 March 2023. Reproduced by permission of the BBC History Extra; **Florence Sutcliffe-Braithwaite:** 'The 1967 Sexual Offences Act: a landmark moment in the history of British homosexuality', BBC History Extra, 14 July 2018. Reproduced by permission of the BBC History Extra; **Peter Tatchell:** 'Idealism, Pride and Anger - The Beginnings of Lesbian and Gay Liberation in Britain', published by Capital Gay, 23 June 1989. Reproduced by permission of Peter Tatchell Foundation; **Tim Tate:** *Pride: The Unlikely Story of the True Heroes of the Miner's Strike*, published by John Blake Publishing Limited. Reproduced by permission of Bonnier Books UK; **Alex Taylor:** 'Spice Girls: What happened to Girl Power?', published by BBC News. Reproduced with permission of BBC News at bbc.co.uk/news; **Alex Wheatle:** ''We felt that we didn't belong' - Alex Wheatle tells his story of the Brixton Riots'. Reproduced with permission of BBC News at bbc.co.uk/news; **Alex Wheatle:** 'Alex Wheatle interview' from 'Brixton Riot' collection (2009) © Museum of London. Reproduced with permission of Museum of London.

Photos: p6(t): Topical Press Agency / Stringer / Getty Images; **p6(b):** Trinity Mirror / Mirrorpix / Alamy Stock Photo; **p7(t):** Copyright unknown; **p7(b):** Trinity Mirror / Mirrorpix / Alamy Stock Photo; **p8:** Glasgow City Archives; **p9:** Chronicle / Alamy Stock Photo; **p10:** IanDagnall Computing / Alamy Stock Photo; **p11:** TOLGA AKMEN/AFP via Getty Images; **p12(t):** Trinity Mirror / Mirrorpix / Alamy Stock Photo; **p12(b):** akg-images / Erich Lessing; **p14:** Trinity Mirror / Mirrorpix / Alamy Stock Photo; **p15:** Christopher Tollast / Alamy Stock Photo; **p16(l):** Allan Cash Picture Library / Alamy Stock Photo; **p16(r):** Pictorial Press Ltd / Alamy Stock Photo; **p17:** PA Photos / TopFoto; **p18:** Trinity Mirror / Mirrorpix / Alamy Stock Photo; **p19(l):** Copyright unknown; **p19(r):** Copyright unknown; **p21:** Mirrorpix / Contributor; **p23:** PA Images / Alamy Stock Photo; **p24:** Alyssa Milano; **p25:** © Angela Christofilou/The Independent ; **p26:** Chronicle / Alamy Stock Photo; **p28:** Working Class Movement Library; **p29(t):** Guy Corbishley / Alamy Stock Photo; **p29(b):** Disabled People's Archive; **p30:** General Photographic Agency / Stringer; **p31:** Bristol Collections; **p32:** IanDagnall Computing / Alamy Stock Photo; **p33:** Courtesy of Royal Greenwich Heritage Trust; **p34(t):** American Printing House for the Blind, Inc., M.C. Migel Library; **p34(b):** Working Class Movement Library; **p37:** © LCD; **p38:** Crippencartoons.com; **p39:** Keystone Press / Alamy Stock Photo; **p40:** Disabled People's Archive; **p41:** Guy Corbishley / Alamy Stock Photo; **p42(t):** David Grimwade / Alamy Stock Photo; **p42(b):** © Crown copyright. Historic England Archive; **p43:** G.P.Essex / Alamy Stock Photo; **p44:** Open Parliament Licence v3.0; **p46:** © People's History Museum; **p47:** Greater Manchester Coalition of Disabled People, sourced from the Disabled People's Archive; **p48:** G.P.Essex / Alamy Stock Photo; **p49:** © Victoria and Albert Museum, London, 2023/Purchased through the Julie and Robert Breckman Print Fund; **p50(tl):** Daily Herald Archive / Contributor / Getty Images; **p50(tr):** Trinity Mirror / Mirrorpix / Alamy Stock Photo; **p50(b):** Steve Taylor ARPS / Alamy Stock Photo; **p51(l):** © 2023 Goldsmiths, University of London; **p51(m):** Allstar Picture Library Ltd / Alamy Stock Photo; **p51(r):** Dave Bagnall / Alamy Stock Photo; **p52:** Daily Herald Archive / Contributor / Getty Images; **p54:** FPG / Staff; **p55:** Trinity Mirror / Mirrorpix / Alamy Stock Photo; **p56:** Charlie Gillett Collection / Contributor; **p57:** Imageplotter / Alamy Stock Photo; **p59:** Pictorial Press Ltd / Alamy Stock Photo; **p60:** Independent / Alamy Stock Photo; **p61:** Steve Taylor ARPS / Alamy Stock Photo; **p63:** Tony Byers / Alamy Stock Photo; **p64:** Shakeyjon / Alamy Stock Photo; **p66(l):** PA Images / Alamy Stock Photo; **p66(r):** PA Images / Alamy Stock Photo; **p67(l):** Dave Bagnall / Alamy Stock Photo; **p67(m):** Allstar Picture Library Ltd / Alamy Stock Photo; **p67(r):** © 2023 Goldsmiths, University of London; **p68:** David Hoffman; **p70:** Imageplotter / Alamy Stock Photo; **p73(t):** LEON NEAL / Getty Images; **p73(m):** Colin Clews; **p73(b):** © 2023 Bishopsgate Foundation; **p75(l):** Joseph Gaul / Alamy Stock Photo; **p75(r):** Copyright unknown; **p76(l):** Used under CC BY SA 3.0; **p76(r):** © 2023 Glasgow Women's Library; **p77:** PA Images / Alamy Stock Photo; **p78:** Everett Collection, Inc. / Alamy Stock Photo; **p79(l):** Dimple Patel / Alamy Stock Photo; **p79(r):** Dimple Patel / Alamy Stock Photo; **p80:** © 2023 Bishopsgate Foundation; **p81:** Jamie Gardiner; **p83:** Andreas Hansen; **p84:** Colin Clews; **p85:** Contraband Collection / Alamy Stock Photo; **p86(l):** Carl Austin-Behan; **p86(r):** Mark Waugh; **p87:** LEON NEAL / Getty Images; **p88(t):** Allstar Picture Library Ltd / Alamy Stock Photo; **p88(b):** © West Bromwich Albion's LGBTQ+ supporters club; **p89:** Sampajano_Anizza/Shutterstock; **p90:** Joe Slater/Shutterstock; **p91:** ZUMA Press, Inc. / Alamy Stock Photo; **p92:** Jamie Gardiner.

Artwork by Chanté Timothy, Darley Anderson Illustration Agency.

Every effort has been made to contact copyright holders of material reproduced in this book. Any omissions will be rectified in subsequent printings if notice is given to the publisher.

Links to third party websites are provided by Oxford in good faith and for information only. Oxford disclaims any responsibility for the materials contained in any third party website referenced in this work.

The publisher would like to thank the following people for offering their contribution in the development of this book: Abigail Woodman, David Rawlings, James Helling, Vicky Iglikowski-Broad, Beckie Rutherford, Rosa Legeno-Bell, Mark Wilson and Jenny Mabbott. The publisher would also like to thank the following people for their careful review of relevant sections: Dr Stella Moss, Beckie Rutherford, Dr Ayshah Johnston, Dr Justin Bengry, Mark Wilson, Dr Shirin Hirsch and Tony Stevens.

From the authors

Lindsay Bruce: To Chris and Jean – my world. And to the learners at Penn Hall School.

Rebecca Carter: Thank you to Dan, James, Ben, Rachel, the humanities team, and the school LGBTQ+ student group for all their support and inspiration.

Alex Fairlamb: For my beautiful mum. The fiercest, strongest woman who inspires me endlessly.

Teni Gogo: Thank you to Eric, the team at Ark Pioneer and Jubilee.

Dan Lyndon-Cohen: Thank you to Monty Shield for his insight, wisdom and knowledge and Maggie for being such an inspiring role model for LGBTQ+ rights in schools.

Josh Preye Garry: Thank you to my wife Lizzy, mother and Brother KG for all the support, and the people of Brixton for letting me tell their story.

Aaron Wilkes: Thank you to Abigail Woodman, Alison Schrecker and Beth Kamen at OUP, and to the team at the People's History Museum in Manchester.

Contents

Introducing KS3 History: Fight for Rights

What is this book about?

We all have rights: things we are entitled to. Today, in Britain these rights include the right to education, the right to vote once you have reached the age of 18, and the right to a fair trial if you have been charged with a crime. It is easy to take these rights for granted and to assume that your parents, grandparents and great grandparents had them too. But almost all the rights we enjoy today have been fought for. People who identified an injustice, or experienced the same injustice, came together to demand their rights; to demand change.

In this textbook you will be introduced to the fascinating history of four fights for rights: the fight for Women's Rights, the fight for Disability Rights, the fight for Black Civil Rights and the fight for LGBTQ+ Rights. You will meet lots of interesting people along the way, who have worked together to make Britain fairer and more equal. You will also learn that in all four cases the fight for rights, for equality, is not yet over.

While you're reading, try to remember that although people with similar experiences come together to fight for their rights, everyone's lives are unique. This means that your experiences may not be the same as the people you meet in these pages, or the same as the person next to you. We've had to make some difficult decisions about what to leave out. Nevertheless, we hope you see how your life connects to the lives of those who have fought for their rights in modern Britain. You may be a woman, you may be disabled, you may be Black, you may be lesbian, gay, bisexual or transgender, or you may be an ally. An ally is someone who fights for rights on behalf of a group despite not belonging to the group, and allies play a very important role in challenging the existing state of affairs. We can all choose to be allies!

Using this book

This book will get you thinking. Some of the things you look at will challenge you. Some things might really surprise you, or get you thinking in a different way. You will be asked to look at different pieces of evidence and to try to work out things for yourself. Sometimes, we do not have lots of evidence and you might be asked to think of reasons why this is. Your answers might not be the same as your friend's or even your teacher's. This is okay. The important thing is to give reasons for your thoughts and ideas.

Getting the history right

We have consulted lots of experts to ensure that the content of this book is as accurate as possible and reflects the latest 'historical scholarship' (historians writing about history). Historians who have helped us include Dr Stella Moss (Royal Holloway, University of London), Beckie Rutherford (University of Warwick), Dr Ayshah Johnston (Black Cultural Archives) and Dr Justin Bengry (Centre for Queer History at Goldsmiths, University of London). We are extremely grateful for all the support and guidance from the People's History Museum, Manchester, particularly in shaping the Disability Rights chapter. We have also worked with Rosa Legeno-Bell (Diverse History UK), Tony Stevens (Disability Rights UK), Arthur Torrington (Windrush Foundation) and Vicky Iglikowski-Broad (Principal Records Specialist: Diverse Histories at The National Archives).

There's another thing that's important to mention when we study the fight for rights – the story isn't fixed. It is constantly developing as historians think more deeply about this area and uncover rich stories about the people who were (and still are) involved in the fight. We've also tried really hard to ensure that the voices of people who have lived these experiences are at the heart of this book, so you get an authentic perspective of the way the issues, events and developments have made an impact on their lives. However, it is sometimes very difficult to find out how people in the past would describe themselves. We are aware that people have multi-layered identities and that the ways we have chosen to describe them may not be the way they would have chosen to describe themselves. We hope we've managed to show you a thorough picture.

Aaron, Alex, Becky, Dan, Josh, Lindsay and Teni

Key to features

Objectives All enquiries in this book start by setting you objectives. These are your key aims setting out your learning targets for the work ahead.

Key Words These are important words and terms that are vital to your understanding of the topic. You can spot them easily because they are in bold red type. Look up their meanings in the glossary at the back of the book.

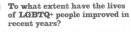

Fact ✓ These are fascinating little bits of history that you don't usually hear about! They sometimes provide extra information that challenge the way you think. They're important because they give you extra insights into topics.

Over to You .ıll These activities are an opportunity for you to demonstrate your knowledge and understanding of the history you've been learning. In each box the tasks become progressively more challenging.

Earlier on... / Meanwhile... / Later on... You will be challenged to think how the topic you are studying relates to events, people, ideas or developments in fights for rights that happened many years before, that took place at the same time, or that occurred many years later.

Connections 🔗 These give you an idea of what is happening in other fights for rights in Britain, and also in other parts of the world, at the same sort of time as the fight you are studying in the lesson. They will help you draw parallels between fights.

History Skills ⭐ These activities test a range of history skills, so each box has its own title. The tasks will challenge you to think a little deeper about what you have been studying. These are also important skills to develop if you are going to study GCSE History.

Have you been learning?

There are different types of assessments at the end of every chapter. These are opportunities for you to showcase what you have learned and to put your ability to recall key information and demonstrate history skills to the test.

Quick Knowledge Quiz These short tests will give you a quick snapshot of what you have

In-depth activities These activities will test your knowledge and understanding of the chapter in more depth. They will also help you develop key skills such as making inferences and writing in detail.

1 The fight for Women's Rights

Introduction

At the beginning of the twentieth century, a large gap separated men and women in the UK. Women who worked were paid less than men. Many professions (such as teaching) expected women to leave their jobs when they got married: their place was thought to be in the home, looking after their husbands and children. And women could not vote in general elections to choose the Members of Parliament (MPs) who ran the country. Today, the picture is very different: women are MPs, they run companies and they have reached the highest levels of most professions. These changes did not happen automatically, however. Women had to fight for every single one of these rights. You are going to find out how women secured the right to vote in general elections, and how women fought for social equality (for equal rights and equal status). You are also going to find out if the Acts of Parliament that ensure women are treated equally to men mean the fight for Women's Rights has been won.

We are going to start with a timeline of the main events in the story of the fight for Women's Rights.

KEY

The fight for Women's Rights is divided into stages or 'waves'. This book covers four waves of the fight.

- ● First-wave feminism
- ■ Second-wave feminism
- ▲ Third-wave feminism
- ★ Fourth-wave feminism

1910
On 18 November, suffragettes organise a demonstration in Parliament Square. There are violent clashes between the protestors and police. The day becomes known as Black Friday.

1914–1918
The First World War takes place and many women directly support the war effort.

1918
The Representation of the People Act is passed. All men over the age of 21 and women over the age of 30 who are householders, or who own property, secure the right to vote in general elections.

1897
The National Union of Women's Suffrage Societies (NUWSS) is formed. It is led by Millicent Fawcett. Members become known as the suffragists.

1928
The Representation of the People (Equal Franchise) Act is passed. All women over the age of 21 are given the vote; men and women now have equal rights to vote in general elections.

1903
The Women's Social and Political Union (WSPU) is formed. It is led by Emmeline Pankhurst. Members become known as the suffragettes.

1939–1945
The Second World War takes place and many women directly support the war effort.

1990s

Girl Power erupts into mainstream music in the 1990s. The Spice Girls are the most famous example.

2017

Actor Alyssa Milano's tweet about her experiences of sexual harassment sparks the #MeToo Movement.

1989

Kimberlé Crenshaw first uses the term 'intersectionality' to describe how individual characteristics – like sex, class, race and sexual orientation – connect with each other.

1977

The first Reclaim the Night march takes place in Leeds. It is a women-only march against sexual violence and for gender equality, and it continues today.

1975

The Sex Discrimination Act is passed. It is now illegal to discriminate against women and men because of their sex or whether or not they are married. Discrimination is the unjust treatment of people because they belong to a particular group; people experience discrimination for many reasons, including race, gender, gender identity, sexual orientation and disability.

1976

Women at the Grunwick Film Processing Laboratories go on strike, led by Jayaben Desai. Their demands include better working conditions, an end to compulsory overtime, and an end to discrimination in the workplace.

1970

The Women's Liberation Movement holds its first meeting.

The Equal Pay Act is passed. It is now illegal to pay women less than men for doing the same job.

The Women's Liberation Front protest at the Miss World pageant in London.

1968

Working-class female sewing machinists go on strike at the Ford factory in Dagenham. They are demanding equal pay for equal work.

abortion (end a pregnancy) within strict rules.

1.1 How did women secure the right to vote?

In 1900, women did not have the same rights as men, and they certainly did not have the same rights as women do today. It was thought that a woman's place was in the home. They could not vote in general elections to choose the MPs who ran the country, and they could not become MPs themselves. Angered by this, women formed organisations to demand change – and it worked. By 1928, all British women over the age of 21 had the right to vote in general elections, just like all British men over the age of 21. But how did women fight to win equal voting rights? What methods did women's organisations use? And what finally convinced men to grant women the right to vote?

Objectives

- Describe why women wanted the right to vote.
- Analyse the methods used by women's organisations in their fight to secure the right to vote.
- Explain the impact of women's work during the First World War on the fight to secure the right to vote.

1.1A The suffragists

'Angel in the house'

At the beginning of the twentieth century, women were expected to be 'angels in the house'. When women married, they promised during the marriage ceremony to 'obey' their husbands. They were expected to replace the surnames they were given at birth with their husbands' surnames. Girls were taught how to look after a home and family: how to cook and clean and manage a household.

Working-class women tended to carry on working after marriage, but they continued to be paid less than men for the same work. The few middle-class women who did have jobs were expected to quit when they got married, to focus on being wives and mothers. This was known as the 'marriage bar'.

Many men and some women thought women were not clever enough to have the vote or understand politics, and that they would make poor decisions when voting.

▶ **SOURCE A** This cartoon, from 1902, shows John Bull (representing the British government) shrugging his shoulders at a woman who is bound and gagged. The gag reads 'voteless' and the binding says things such as 'inequality before the law', 'no financial control' and 'prejudice'.

Connections

As you learn about the fight for rights in modern Britain, you will see the terms 'working class', 'middle class' and 'upper class'. Often, the amount of money you have relates to the opportunities you have to fight for your rights. Working-class people, for example, are generally poorer, so might find it difficult to take time off work to go on protests or on strike, and any fines received as punishment would be far more devastating. The less money a person has, the more vulnerable they (and their children) are if campaigning gets them into trouble.

Meanwhile... 1893

In 1893, New Zealand became the first country in the world to give women the right to vote. From then on, all women in New Zealand could choose who would represent them.

Step forward the suffragists

In 1866, a group of women in Manchester organised a petition calling for a change in the law to allow women to vote. They believed having the vote would enable them to influence wages and working conditions for women, as well as improve the lives of children. However, when a new voting law was introduced a year later, more men gained the vote but not women!

In response, a new, national organisation was established in 1897, led by Millicent Fawcett. It brought together lots of different suffrage societies and was called the National Union of Women's Suffrage Societies (the NUWSS). Suffrage means the right to vote: the members became known as the suffragists and red, green and white became their movement's colours.

The suffragists used peaceful tactics to gain support. They knew that the people against rights for women would accuse them of

The Great Pilgrimage

The most famous suffragist march was the Great Pilgrimage in 1913. Over the course of six weeks, people walked across Britain to meet in Hyde Park in London for a big demonstration. Along the way they held meetings to spread the word. The Great Pilgrimage was in response to a challenge the Prime Minster at the time, Herbert Asquith, had set Millicent Fawcett: 'I will listen to you, if you can prove that "ordinary women" want the vote.' Although the marchers met with some opposition, they successfully proved that people all over the country wanted women to have the vote.

▼ **SOURCE B** A photograph of the Great Pilgrimage suffragists marching towards Hyde Park in 1913.

Progress by 1914

The suffragists had 54,000 members by 1912 and they had raised the profile of the campaign for votes for women, but women still did not have the vote. Then in 1914, when the First World War broke out, the suffragists put down their petitions and focused on supporting the war effort.

Over to You

1 Describe the rights and roles the majority of women had at the start of the twentieth century.

2 a Explain why the suffragists chose legal, peaceful methods to campaign for votes for women.

b Which of the campaigning methods that the suffragists used do you think would have been most effective? Explain your answer in

1.1B The suffragettes

Deeds not words!

After decades of campaigning for votes for women, many people were frustrated at the lack of progress. They felt that the suffragists' tactics did not bring enough attention to the cause. So, in 1903, they formed the Women's Social and Political Union (the WSPU). The *Daily Mail* newspaper quickly nicknamed them the suffragettes.

The suffragettes had the same aim as the suffragists – they wanted to persuade the government to give women the right to vote – and many suffragists joined them. However, the suffragettes had very different tactics. Led by Emmeline Pankhurst and her daughters, the suffragettes added confrontational and militant (violent) campaigning methods to the legal, peaceful campaigning methods used by the suffragists. The fight for women's right to vote was, for them, a war. Their battle cry was 'Deeds not words'!

▼ **SOURCE C** In 1913, Christabel Pankhurst, one of Emmeline Pankhurst's daughters, explained the suffragettes' militant approach.

'If men use explosives and bombs for their own purpose, they call it war and the throwing of a bomb that destroys other people is then described as a glorious and heroic deed. Why should a woman not make use of the same weapons as men? It is not only war we have declared. We are fighting for a revolution!'

Black Friday

The suffragettes' approach to protest hardened after what became known as Black Friday. In 1910, the suffragettes organised a demonstration in Parliament Square. Instead of arresting the demonstrators, there were violent clashes and reports of women being beaten and sexually assaulted by police. The suffragettes came to believe the government cared more for property than for the lives of women, so they decided to fight even harder to win the vote and to focus more on destroying property.

Connections

Rosa May Billinghurst was a suffragette involved in the Black Friday demonstration. She was a wheelchair user and described how police threw her out of her wheelchair. There are also reports of her driving her wheelchair at the police.

Sophia Duleep Singh was another suffragette involved in the Black Friday demonstration. She was the daughter of the last Maharaja of the Sikh Empire in India, and Queen Victoria's goddaughter.

Smashing windows and setting fires

In 1911 and 1912, the suffragettes organised two window-smashing campaigns, targeting shops and offices in the West End of London. Then, between 1913 and 1914, they carried out hundreds of bombings and arson attacks, deliberately destroying and setting fire to buildings. There were 52 arson attacks in May 1913 alone and, in the same month, they attempted to bomb St Paul's Cathedral.

▼ **SOURCE D** A photograph of the Tea House in Kew Gardens in London after it was burned to the ground by suffragettes Lilian Lenton and Olive Wharry in February 1913.

Hunger strikes in prison

The suffragettes knew what they were doing was illegal and that they could be sent to prison. When in prison, some went on hunger strike, refusing to eat any food. Initially, the government released hunger strikers, but soon decided to force feed them instead. A rubber tube was forced down the noses or throats and into the stomachs of women who refused to eat, and food was poured down the tube. This was a painful and terrifying experience, which caused many injuries. Over 1,000 women were force fed in this way, some many times.

Reports in the press about force feeding gained the suffragettes sympathy. In response, the government passed the Prisoners (Temporary Discharge for Ill-Health) Act in 1913. Suffragettes on hunger strike were temporarily let out of prison until they recovered, and then they had to return. The suffragettes nicknamed the Act the 'Cat and Mouse Act', saying the government was like a cat playing with a mouse, catching it and letting it go over and over again.

▶ **SOURCE E** Suffragettes were awarded a medal for going on hunger strike. The ribbon is green, white and purple, the suffragette colours, which stand for hope, purity and loyalty.

Reactions to the suffragettes' methods

For over one hundred years, the methods used by the suffragettes have been criticised by some and celebrated by others.

▼ **INTERPRETATION F** In this adapted extract from a 2018 British Library online article, historian Fern Riddell explains how many were turned off by the suffragettes' militant tactics.

'The WSPU acted like an army with professional soldiers, seeing the period as a civil war between the

▼ **INTERPRETATION G** In a 1958 children's history book, Edward Boyd celebrates the courage of the suffragettes.

'The suffragette movement developed into a tremendous force. Its increase of numbers made it no longer possible for its enemies to dismiss it as the cranky notion of a few women. The suffragettes were helped, too, rather than hindered by the stupidity and brutality of those in authority. Time and again these brave women were sent to prison where they were treated with less consideration than the commonest and vilest criminal. When they went on hunger strike, they were forcibly fed. A great many people, who had not cared one way or the other about votes for women, changed their minds when they learned of such indignities.'

Progress by 1914

When the First World War broke out, the suffragettes started negotiating with the government. When the government released all suffragettes from prison, the WSPU largely suspended its campaigning to help with the war effort.

Over to You

1   How did the methods used by the suffragettes to campaign for votes for women differ from the methods used by the suffragists?

2   Write a sentence or two explaining what the suffragettes meant by 'Deeds not words'.

3   Explain why the suffragettes chose confrontational, militant and often illegal methods to campaign for votes for women.

1.1C The First World War and votes for women

Contributing to the war effort

When the First World War broke out in July 1914, millions of men quickly joined up to fight. Many women, including most suffragists and suffragettes, wanted to help too. However, the government was slow to use women to fill the jobs that men had left behind. Emmeline and Christabel Pankhurst launched into action! They put pressure on MPs and organised rallies to persuade the government to let women play their part.

▼ **INTERPRETATION H** An extract from Christabel Pankhurst's book, *Unshackled: The story of how we won the vote*, published in 1959.

'Mother and I declared support of our country. We declared an armistice [a truce] with the Government and suspended militancy for the duration of the war. We offered our service to the country and called upon all members to do likewise. As Mother said, "What would be the good of a vote without a country to vote in!"'

Eventually, the government changed its mind. Women went to work in jobs that they had not been allowed to do before. By 1918, more than one million women from all social classes were at work. And they proved that they were strong enough and clever enough to do work that had previously been 'men's work'.

- Women worked in factories making weapons, and as bus drivers, conductors and mechanics.
- Women joined the Women's Land Army, working on farms to keep the country fed.
- Women joined the Voluntary Aid Detachment and the First Aid Nursing Yeomanry, travelling to the Western Front to nurse wounded soldiers.
- Women supported the armed forces, joining the Women's Army Auxiliary Corps and the Women's Royal Naval Service.

▼ **SOURCE I** A photograph of women making bombs in 1916. The work was dangerous, and it is thought that around 60 women died from poisoning and many more from explosions. Then, at the end of a long day, many women also had to return home to look after their children.

Endell Street Military Hospital

Flora Murray and Louisa Garrett Anderson were qualified doctors, suffragettes and life partners. When the British government told women they could not help with the war effort, Murray and Garrett Anderson travelled to France and set up two hospitals to treat wounded soldiers. The hospitals were so successful that the Royal Army Medical Corps asked them to open Endell Street Military Hospital in London in 1915. This was the first female-run hospital in Britain, and it had treated about 26,000 patients by the end of the war.

▶ **SOURCE J** A painting of Murray and Garrett Anderson operating on a patient at the Endell Street Military Hospital. It was painted in 1920 by Francis Dodd, who was an Official War Artist during the First World War.

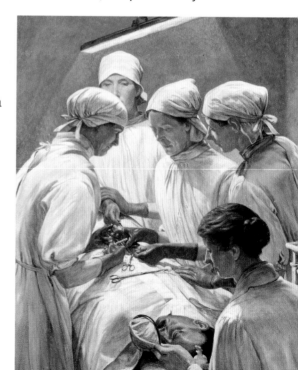

Changing attitudes

As the war continued and more women went to work, attitudes towards women having the vote began to change. By the end of the war, it was widely recognised that women had helped win the war. Their effort, determination and skill helped change people's minds about what women were capable of. Some even felt they had 'proved themselves worthy' of the vote.

▼ **INTERPRETATION K** Diane Atkinson, writing in her 1996 book *The Suffragettes in Pictures*, explains the impact that women working during the First World War had on attitudes towards women having the vote.

'Women from all social classes helped to "keep the home fires burning" and joined in the war effort. An enormous range of semi-skilled and labouring jobs had been taken up by women, who had previously not been allowed, or not considered themselves able to do such work. By the end of the war, women had demonstrated they were not weak, frail, unintelligent creatures. They had helped to win the war, and at the same time, overturned society's views about men's and women's roles.'

Women get the right to vote at last!

The 1918 Representation of the People Act gave the vote to all men over the age of 21, and to women over the age of 30 who were householders or who owned property. This was a significant step forward: it meant that 40 per cent of women now had the vote. But it did not result in equality between men and women: over 12.5 million women (most of them working-class and young women) still could not choose who represented them in Parliament. Suffrage campaigners continued to demand equality with men. Eventually, in 1928, the Representation of the People (Equal Franchise) Act was passed and all women over 21 were given the right to vote.

The activities of the suffragists and the suffragettes, alongside the work women did during the First World War, led to women securing the right to vote. The suffragist and the suffragettes b...

▼ **INTERPRETATION L** In a 2018 talk for the National Archives, historian Fern Riddell explains why she believes the government gave women the right to vote. This extract of the talk has been adapted.

'So as far as the public was concerned, I think, the suffragettes' militancy was dangerous, but as far as the government was concerned there was a very different pressure. At the end of the First World War, there was a serious fear that the militancy would kick off again and the government, attempting to put the country back together again after the war, desperately needed to make sure that things were as calm as possible. And I personally believe that's one of the reasons why women were granted the vote.'

Meanwhile... 1918

The 1918 Parliament (Qualification of Women) Act allowed women to become MPs. Constance Markievicz (an Irish politician) was the first woman elected as a British MP in 1918, but she refused to take her seat because she did not want to swear an oath of allegiance to the monarch. Nancy Astor was the second woman elected to Parliament and she took her seat in 1919. It's interesting that women under the age of 30 could become MPs even though, at this point in time, they were not allowed to vote!

Over to You

1 Why were the suffragists and the suffragettes willing to suspend their campaigns for votes for women and help with the war eff...

Why did women demand social equality?

By 1928, all men and women over the age of 21 could vote, and women could become MPs. Women had secured political equality with men. But the fight for Women's Rights was far from over. Socially, women were still considered inferior to men. Women were expected to get married and focus on looking after their families. If they worked, women were paid less than men. The Second World War changed very little, and in the 1960s women started to loudly demand social equality. Why did the Second World War fail to deliver the leap forward in Women's Rights that the First World War had? How did women fight for the right to make decisions about their own bodies in the 1960s and 1970s? And how did women fight for equality in the workplace?

Objectives

- Discuss what life was like for women in Britain in the aftermath of the Second World War.
- Describe how women gained greater control over their bodies in the 1960s and 1970s.
- Explain how women fought for equality in the workplace in the 1960s and 1970s.

1.2A Women went back to the kitchen at the end of the Second World War

The legacy of the First World War

It is widely recognised that the work women did during the First World War (1914–1918) had a major impact in helping women secure equal voting rights with men in 1928. This was a significant step in the fight for Women's Rights. So, it would seem logical to assume that after the Second World War (1939–1945), when women once more rose to the challenge, there would be another breakthrough.

Contributing to the war effort during the Second World War

When the Second World War broke out in 1939, it presented another opportunity to disprove the stereotype that women were weak. They demonstrated their strength, skill and bravery by, for example, working in factories making planes, joining the Women's Land Army to grow food, and joining the Women's Royal Army Corps, the Women's Royal Naval Service and the Women's Royal Air Force. At the same time, those who were mothers continued to look after their children.

Fact ✓

Women in the Women's Land Army were known as 'land girls'. They were paid around 25 per cent less than the men who worked alongside them doing the same jobs!

▼ **SOURCE A** The Women's Timber Corps was part of the Women's Land Army. People who worked in the Corps were nicknamed 'lumberjills'. This photograph of two lumberjills guiding a tree trunk through a saw was taken in 1945.

A woman's place is back in the home

The Second World War had a long-lasting impact on British society, and two developments in particular had an impact on the lives of girls and women:

- The 1944 Education Act introduced free secondary education for all pupils, which meant that more girls could gain the qualifications they needed to broaden their career opportunities.
- The 1946 National Health Service Act introduced free healthcare for all. Before the creation of the National Health Service (NHS), most poorer women had been unable to afford to visit a doctor or pay for medication. Now they could access medical treatment and experience relief from painful conditions they had suffered with for years.

However, day-to-day life for women after the Second World War was generally similar to life before the war. When men were released from the armed forces, they came back to Britain and returned to their jobs. This meant women had little choice but to go back to the lives they had had before the war too – cooking and cleaning, and looking after their husbands and children.

▼ **SOURCE B** This advert from the 1950s puts pressure on women to be the perfect wives and mothers, reinforcing sexist stereotypes.

"The Kenwood you bought me prepared this wonderful meal"

WITH A KENWOOD in the kitchen, cooking

Key Words   stereotype

The newly formed advertising industry played a big part in reinforcing sexist roles. Adverts for items like washing-up liquid, food mixers and washing machines were aimed at women to emphasise their roles as 'perfect housewives'. Magazines were published for women that focused on hair and make-up, recipes and knitting patterns, to help women keep themselves and their homes looking nice for their husbands.

▼ **INTERPRETATION C** In March 2013, Zoe Fairbairns talked to the British Library about being a young woman in the late 1950s and early 1960s.

'It seemed to me that as a grown woman, one of two things was going to happen to you. Either you were going to get married, in which case you would be miserable for the rest of your life, because you would be expected to give everything up or at least put it second. Or, alternatively, you would fail to get married, in which case — although maybe you would have some freedom and a nice career, and maybe your own home — you would still be viewed as a failure and faintly ridiculous because you had failed in the most important thing, which was to get a man.'

Over to You

1 a There was progress in Women's Rights after the First World War. Write a sentence describing what happened and why.

   b Did Women's Rights make similar progress after the Second World War? Write a sentence describing what happened and why.

2 Analyse **Source B**.

   a What impression does the advert give about ho...

1.2B Women fight for the right to control their bodies

Second-wave feminism

After the Second World War and throughout the 1950s, women campaigned for social equality (for equal rights and equal status), particularly for equal pay. Then, in the 1960s, the campaign increased in intensity. Some women started calling themselves feminists, and argued for economic, social and political equality between men and women. They drew a distinction between first-wave feminists (the people who campaigned for the right to vote between 1897 and 1928) and second-wave feminists (their campaign for social equality). They acknowledged that they owed a significant debt of gratitude to the first-wave feminists, and particularly to the suffragists and the suffragettes.

The second-wave feminists – often referred to as the Women's Liberation Movement (Women's Lib) – used some of the tactics used by the first-wave feminists. For example, they organised protests and they smashed windows. But they also used new tactics, taking advantage of developments in the media to get their message across to a wide audience.

Freedom through fashion

Women began to express themselves through their clothes. Feminists encouraged women to make fashion choices that made them feel good about themselves, and to stop wearing the clothes and hairstyles that had traditionally been expected.

In the 1950s, women were expected to wear modest 'feminine' clothing. In the 1960s, dresses and skirts became much shorter and women experimented with their hairstyles and the make-up they wore. In the 1970s, more women wore trousers.

Choosing when to have children

Until the 1960s, it was difficult for sexually active women to control when they had children. Some married women were exhausted bearing child after child, and many unmarried women who became pregnant were afraid of being abandoned by their families. It was traditional for a woman to be married before she gave birth and widely viewed as shameful to have a child without being married. A few felt they had no choice but to seek a medical procedure that ends a pregnancy (known as an abortion).

▼ SOURCE D
A photograph of British housewives in the 1950s.

▼ SOURCE E
A photograph showing two women wearing miniskirts, short hair and heavy eye make-up in 1965.

However, abortions were banned at this time. They were performed illegally, sometimes by untrained people. These 'backstreet abortions' were extremely dangerous and could result in serious illness and even death.

In 1961, the contraceptive pill was introduced for married women. This was revolutionary: for the first time, women were able to choose whether or not they wanted to have a baby. However, second-wave feminists were angry that unmarried women did not have access to the pill. They wanted all women to be able to enjoy sex without fear of getting pregnant and they campaigned tirelessly for a change in the law. They won! In 1967, the contraceptive pill was made available to all women. In the same year, the 1967 Abortion Act was also passed. It was now legal for medical professionals to perform an abortion within strict rules.

Fact ✓

Many women celebrated the pill and the legalisation of abortion, because they now had control over their own bodies. However, not all women welcomed these changes. Today, pro-life groups campaign against abortion and pro-choice groups campaign for abortion.

▼ **INTERPRETATION F** In this adapted extract, Nishah Malik, Collections Editor at the British Archives Online, explains the importance of the contraceptive pill in an online article published in 2022.

'The introduction of the contraceptive pill was a milestone moment for the women's liberation movement. Despite some backlash, many women began taking the pill and the usage rose from 50,000 to 1 million between 1962 and 1969. Women could now enjoy sex, and continue their careers or education without the fear of getting pregnant.'

Flour power!

Despite many women, and particularly many young women, being able to choose more freely what they wore, there was still lots of sexism in the 1960s and 1970s. The media continued to present women as objects to be looked at by men. One example of this was the Miss World pageant.

Miss World started in London in 1951 and it still continues today. Women from all over the world compete each year and are judged on what they look like, what they wear and how they present themselves. In 1970 a group from the Women's Liberation Movement were so angry about what was happening that they planned a protest.

They bought tickets and sat in the audience. Then, when a pre-agreed signal was given, they threw flour bombs and stink bombs at the host, blew whistles and shouted, 'We're not beautiful. We're not ugly. We're angry!' Millions around the world were watching the pageant on television and saw the protest.

In 1971, the Women's Liberation Movement was fighting for equal pay, education and job opportunities; free contraception and abortion on demand; and free 24-hour nurseries.

▶ **SOURCE G** A photograph of a Miss World protestor outside the Royal Albert Hall in 1970.

Key Words   feminists
first-wave feminists   second-wave feminists
sexism   activists

▼ **INTERPRETATION H** In this adapted extract from a 2023 BBC History Revealed article, Mel Sherwood writes about the impact of the 1970 Miss World protest.

'In November of 1970, anyone watching the Miss World contest would have been presented with a different spectacle to the one scheduled. Activists descended upon the Royal Albert Hall, the venue for the pageant, to disrupt the event in protest of the way it objectified women. Though the press coverage of the protest and the trials that followed was incredibly negative, Women's Lib had never been so popular. Just a few months later, on 6 March 1971, 4,000 women took to London's streets for the first Women's Lib march.'

Over to You

1 Define the following terms in your own words.
   - feminism
   - Women's Liberation Movement

2 a Compare **Sources D** and **E** and list four differences between the photographs.

   b Explain one reason why fashion was an important way for women to challenge stereotypes.

3 Which do you think had the greatest impact on the fight for Women's Rights in the 1960s and 1970s? Explain your decision in no more than 100 words.
   - More freedom for women to choose what they wore.
   - The introduction of the contraceptive pill and the legalisation of abortion.
   - Awareness-raising actions like the 1970 Miss World protest.

1.2C Equal pay for equal work

In Britain, as in most other countries, women are generally paid less than men, even when they do the same job. In the 1960s and 1970s, as women gained more social freedoms and more women went out to work, they began to demand equal pay for equal work. They wanted to be paid the same as men doing the same job, a similar job, an equivalent job, or a job of equal value. However, by 1969 only 18 per cent of women received equal pay.

One way for workers to convince their employer to increase their wages or to improve working conditions is to go out on strike. They get together and refuse to work, in the hope that they will change the balance of power and their employer will have to respond to their demands. Two famous strikes took place in the 1960s and 1970s, both demanding equal pay for women.

Ford machinists strike

In 1968, a group of female sewing machinists went on strike at the Ford car factory in Dagenham in East London. They made car seat covers. This was a skilled Category C job, but the bosses downgraded it to a less-skilled Category B job. The women were also paid 15 per cent less than male colleagues doing Category B jobs. The fight was on.

The women went on strike on 7 June 1968 and were later joined by female machinists at Ford's Halewood factory on Merseyside. Without car seat covers, Ford was unable to finish making cars and production ground to a halt.

Barbara Castle, Labour MP and Secretary of State for Employability and Production, got involved in the strike. She strongly supported equal pay for equal work and her involvement brought an end to the strikes after three weeks. The machinists won an eight per cent wage increase, but were still being paid less than their male colleagues.

▼ **SOURCE I** A photograph of some of the female sewing machinists who went on strike at the Ford factory in Dagenham in 1968.

The strike inspired the formation of the National Joint Action Campaign Committee for Women's Equal Rights. The group held a demonstration in London in 1969 demanding equal pay. Feeling the pressure, Parliament passed the Equal Pay Act in 1970. It became law in 1975 and, from then on, it was illegal to pay women less than men for doing the same job. However, even today there are debates about what 'equal' actually means and women are still campaigning for equality in the workplace.

▼ **INTERPRETATION J** Two extracts from an article written by historian Vicky Iglikowski-Broad, about the impact of the 1968 Ford machinists' strike. The article was published in 2020, on the National Archives website.

'The women workers settled for this agreement. While they did not win their specific demands, they had succeeded in putting huge pressure on the government and giving equal pay a spotlight.'

'[The Equal Pay Act] would not come into force until the end of 1975. In theory this was to give time for rates of pay to be adjusted and financed; in practice it also gave employers time to adjust job descriptions,

1984

The Grunwick strike

Jayaben Desai migrated to the UK in the 1960s from Tanzania. Desai, and many fellow migrants, could only find low-paid jobs when they arrived in Britain. Many went to work at the Grunwick Film Processing Laboratories in 1974.

In August 1976, Desai resigned after being ordered to work overtime at very short notice, and in protest at the way her fellow workers were made to work long hours for low wages. A few days later, she led a walkout: 137 female workers at the lab went on strike. They also joined a trade union, because they realised it would help them fight for their rights. In response, the company started sacking them.

After several months, workers in other trade unions began to support the Grunwick strikers. Soon, trade unionists, students, anti-racist campaigners and feminist groups were standing alongside them outside the lab. On 11 July 1977, over 20,000 people joined them.

However, by the winter of 1977, the trade unions concluded the women could not win the dispute and withdrew their support. The government also sided with the company. Eventually, the strike ended in 1978. Although ultimately unsuccessful, Desai and her fellow strikers had demonstrated that women – and particularly migrant women – were not weak, and that they would stand up for their rights.

Fact ✓

Black and Asian workers had been on strike before the Grunwick dispute and would continue to fight for their rights at work, but this was the first time non-white strikers received trade union support.

▼ **SOURCE K** A photograph of Jayaben Desai during the Grunwick strike (1976), alongside a list of the strikers' objections. A picket, or a picket line, is the group of strikers who stand outside a workplace as a protest.

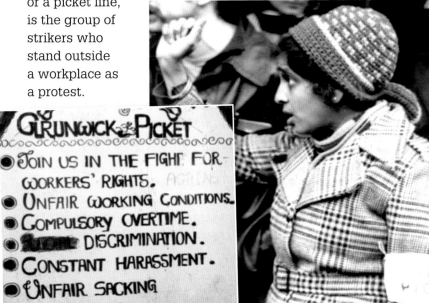

Key Words

visibility   migrants   trade union

▼ **INTERPRETATION L**
Chandrikaben Patel, talking in 2007 about taking part in the Grunwick strike.

'[B]ecause of us, the people who stayed in Grunwick got a much better deal. When the factory moved, the van used to come to their home and pick them up. Can you imagine that?! And they get pension today! And we get nothing. That was because of us, because of our struggle.'

Over to You .ıll

1 a What did the female sewing machinists at the Ford factory in Dagenham make?

  b Why did the machinists go on strike?

  c What was the outcome of the strike? Include 'Halewood factory', 'Barbara Castle' and 'eight per cent' in your answer.

2 Summarise the Grunwick strike in no more than 50 words.

Significance

1 What did the Ford machinists' strike inspire?

2 How effective was the Equal Pay Act of 1970? Did it result in equal pay for women? Explain your answer.

3 Explain the significance of the Ford machinists' strike for equal pay for women.

1.3 Did legal equality result in actual equality?

Women secured equal voting rights with men in 1928. In 1970, it was made illegal to pay women less than men for doing the same job, when the Equal Pay Act was passed. On paper, it looked like women had equal rights with men. However, attitudes were slow to change and the 1975 Sex Discrimination Act was designed to tackle the continuing inequality. Yet movements like the Riot Grrrls and Girl Power in the 1990s, and #MeToo in the 2010s, suggest things are far from equal even today. How effective was the Sex Discrimination Act? What impact did Riot Grrrls and Girl Power have on equality for women? And why was the hashtag #MeToo so momentous?

1.3A The Sex Discrimination Act

The Equal Pay Act fails to live up to expectations

Parliament passed the Equal Pay Act in 1970. It was meant to ensure women were paid the same as men for doing the same job, but it didn't bring about the hoped-for changes. Employers had until 1975 to make the necessary changes, and many used the time to adjust job descriptions so they could continue to pay women less.

Women also faced other forms of discrimination. For example, they weren't offered jobs they were qualified to do, they were passed over for promotions in favour of less-qualified men, and they were expected to work part-time if they were married or had children.

▼ **INTERPRETATION A** Lesley Abdela, a Women's Rights campaigner and journalist, talking about applying for a job before the Sex Discrimination Act was passed in 1975. The interview was recorded in 2013.

'I applied to an ad which I was totally qualified for... so I whacked off an application. And of course I forgot Lesley can be a boy or a girl, man or female. And about a week or so later I get a phone call from somebody who says, "Could I speak to Lesley Abdela?" And I said, "This is Lesley Abdela." "Oh, oh, thought you must be the secretary. Oh, this is a bit awkward. Did you apply for this job we advertised?" and I said, "Yes." "Oh, well we were going to invite you to an interview but we didn't realise you were a woman and I'm awfully sorry but our client wouldn't like a woman."

When they finished school, most young upper-class and middle-class women were expected to become wives and mothers. Women who wanted a career were often viewed as selfish and uncaring. Working-class mothers who had to work were frowned upon because they were not able to stay at home and focus on looking after their children.

The Sex Discrimination Act

Throughout the early 1970s, feminists and feminist organisations put pressure on Parliament to bring an end to discrimination against women. Women in Parliament, including Baroness Seear and Baroness Summerskill, pushed hard for legislation. They met with considerable opposition, but in 1975 the Sex Discrimination Act was passed.

The 1975 Sex Discrimination Act made it illegal to discriminate against women and men because of their sex or whether or not they were married, and the Equal Opportunities Commission was established to make sure such discrimination was acted upon. In the workplace, this meant that women now had the right to equal access to job opportunities and promotions, and to a working environment free from harassment. The right to equal pay was also reinforced.

The 1975 Sex Discrimination Act protected women from discrimination, but it wasn't until the Equality Act was passed in 2010 that men and women were protected from discrimination for a range of other characteristics, such as sexual orientation. Many argue the Sex Discrimination Act paved the way for the Equality Act.

'Terrific' and 'toothless'

The 1975 Sex Discrimination Act was a turning point. For the first time, women were protected from discrimination by law.

▼ **INTERPRETATION B** Anne Morris taught law at a university. In 2017, she wrote about the significance of the Sex Discrimination Act.

'The Sex Discrimination Act 1975 was immensely significant for a whole generation of women who needed no longer to accept that sexism was just the way of the world. They could point to the Act and challenge the discrimination they faced.'

However, the Act didn't have the power to force employers to change. If employers did not change voluntarily, women had to challenge their illegal behaviour in the courts. This meant change was, and still is, slow, leading some critics to refer to the Act as ineffective or 'toothless'.

▶ **SOURCE C**
A photograph of Maureen Colquhoun, Labour politician, in 1980. She felt that the Sex Discrimination Act did not do enough to ensure equality. In 1975 she introduced the Balance of the Sexes Bill to Parliament, which proposed that all public bodies would have to hire an equal number of women and men. However, the Bill did not become law.

▼ **INTERPRETATION D**
A woman shares her experience of the discrimination she suffered because of her sex. She did not want us to publish her name, because she still works in the same industry.

'In 2006, I was 30 years old, unmarried and didn't have children. I worked for a respected company, and I was good at my job. However, things changed when a new manager was appointed. He took a project I was working on away from me, and gave it to a male colleague. He said the male colleague needed the project more because his wife was about to have a baby and they needed to find a way to make sure his job was protected. I was devastated. I thought about challenging the decision legally, but I didn't feel strong enough. Looking back, I wish I had fought harder, and I really admire women who do.'

Over to You

1 Identify two pieces of evidence that suggest the 1970 Equal Pay Act failed to live up to expectations.

2 What can you learn from **Interpretation A** about why the 1975 Sex Discrimination Act was needed?

3 Summarise the 1975 Sex Discrimination Act in two sentences.

4 Read **Interpretation B**, **Source C** and **Interpretation D**. How far do you agree with the argument that the 1975 Sex Discrimination Act was 'toothless'? Write one paragraph agreeing with the view, one paragraph disagreeing with the view, and then a short conclusion stating your opinion.

1.3B Riot Grrrls and Girl Power

Sexism in the 1990s

The 1975 Sex Discrimination Act gave women legal protection against discrimination, but in the early 1990s many women were still experiencing sexism in their daily lives. This was particularly the case for women from ethnic minorities; lesbian, bisexual and transgender women; and disabled women.

▼ **INTERPRETATION F** In 2019, journalist and author Caitlin Moran wrote a magazine article in which she described something that happened to her in the 1990s.

'When I was freelancing for the music press and asked for my first front-page feature, an editor patted his lap and said, "Sit here, let's talk about it." I had absolutely no guide for how to deal with this. It was presented as half-compliment, half-threat. Oh, it was hard to be a girl then! We had not yet really invented the idea of women being, well, humans.'

In response, a new generation of feminists sprang into action in the 1990s. They are sometimes referred to as third-wave feminists. They wanted to smash society's sexist attitudes by empowering women to be individuals and express themselves freely, and they wanted all women to feel part of the fight.

Riot Grrrls

The Riot Grrrl movement combined feminism with punk rock music and politics. It was an underground movement, which means it was self-organised and not part of the mainstream. It began in America in the early 1990s and spread to Britain soon after. Riot Grrrls were frustrated that the patriarchy was still in place. They called out the unfairness of male privilege: the unearned advantages men receive simply because they are men. They were also angry that women still experienced sexism, misogyny, racism and homophobia.

Bands like Bikini Kill, Bratmobile and Le Tigre wrote songs with lyrics that focused on issues that affected women, demanding an end to violence against women, encouraging women to be proud of their bodies and their emotions, and calling for an end to the patriarchy. Young women responded by sharing their experiences and their demands in homemade magazines, called zines, and setting up groups to support victims of sexual violence, racism and homophobia.

Fact ✓

Patriarchy is the system that gives power to men and largely excludes women from power. Sexism is prejudice against women. Misogyny is hatred of women. Racism is prejudice against people from a particular ethnic group, typically a minority ethnic group. Homophobia is prejudice against lesbian, gay or bisexual people.

▼ **SOURCE G** An extract from 'Double Dare Ya', a 1991 song by the Riot Grrrl band Bikini Kill.

'We're Bikini Kill and we want revolution
Girl-style now!

Hey girlfriend
I got a proposition goes something like this:
Dare ya to do what you want
Dare ya to be who you will
Dare ya to cry right out loud
"You get so emotional baby"

Don't you talk out of line
Don't go speaking out of your turn
Gotta listen to what the Man says
Time to make his stomach burn'.

▼ **INTERPRETATION H** An extract from a 2019 article on the *NME* website, which is about music and pop culture.

'Bikini Kill weren't the first female-identifying punk band by any means. But by being so vocal about their political views, the need for women to reclaim their space at shows and in society, and sparking a real revolution in punk and beyond, they opened doors for other women to do the same. They fought the battle to be accepted as a band on their own terms, making it easier for other women and people outside of the white male norm to come in and do what they wanted.'

Girl Power

Girl Power (the title of a Riot Grrrl zine) erupted into mainstream music in the 1990s. Artists such as Queen Latifah challenged the male-dominated world of hip hop, as a rapper and a producer, recording tracks like 'Ladies First'. Girl groups like TLC and Destiny's Child encouraged women to be 'Independent Women' and raised the profile of Black feminism.

Then, in 1996 the Spice Girls arrived on the scene, and Girl Power blared – loud and proud – from radios and televisions across Britain. Each member of the band adopted a different persona to show that feminism was for all women, whatever their personality or style. They wanted to smash the stereotypical idea people had of feminists as unpleasant, unattractive and problematic people. The Spice Girls inspired young women to be confident, and their songs focused on self-respect, consent and friendship.

▼ **SOURCE I** The Spice Girls have had a huge cultural impact. In this photograph, taken in 1997, Sporty Spice, Ginger Spice, Baby Spice, Scary Spice and Posh Spice are seen with Prince Charles (now King Charles III).

Key Words   lesbian   bisexual
transgender   third-wave feminists   patriarchy
misogyny   racism   homophobia   gay   pop culture

▼ **SOURCE K** The Spice Girls talking about feminism in *Girl Power!: The Official Book by the Spice Girls*, which was published in 1997.

'We're freshening up feminism for the nineties. Feminism has become a dirty word. Girl Power is just a nineties way of saying it.'

Over to You

1   Describe Riot Grrrls in under 30 words.

2   What is the difference between 'sexism' and 'misogyny'? Use examples in your answer.

3   Read **Interpretation J**. Identify three reasons O'Connor gives for why the Spice Girls were inspiring.

4   Analyse **Source G**.
   a   What is the key message of the song? Support your answer with a quotation.
   b   The song was written to inspire women, but it was also written to persuade another group of people to behave differently. Who was it trying to persuade and why?

▼ **INTERPRETATION J** Roisin O'Connor is a music journalist. In 2019, she talked to the BBC about the Spice Girls. *Spice*, the group's first album from 1996, has sold 31 million copies worldwide.

'The group have said previously that it was the sexism they faced themselves in the industry that sparked the Girl Power message. Even though every member had to adopt a moniker [name] and fashion persona, this sent a message about individuality. And before that, they were ambitious. They wanted to be famous and successful and they worked hard to achieve that – considering ambition in women is still considered a negative trait, that was another empowering thing to see.'

Knowledge and Understanding

1   Find out more about Bikini Kill and the Spice Girls. How are the two groups different and how are they similar?

2   Explain **one** way in which the role of Bikini Kill and the Spice Girls in the fight for Women's Rights was similar.

1.3C Feminism in the twenty-first century

As the clock struck midnight on 31 December 1999, many hoped the new millennium would signal an end to sexism and misogyny and women would, at long last, feel safe enough to walk the streets alone at night. However, despite the laws and the campaigns of the twentieth century, women are still fighting for equality.

Intersectionality

The term intersectionality was first used by Professor Kimberlé Crenshaw in 1989 to describe how individual characteristics – like gender, class, race and sexual orientation – connect with each other. It helps explain how different people experience something like sexism differently; how a Black working-class woman will experience sexism differently from a white middle-class woman, for example. Feminism as a movement has been criticised for failing to give women from ethnic minorities space to share their experiences. Modern feminism tries to be more inclusive, to ensure feminism is for everybody.

▼ **SOURCE L** Audre Lorde described herself as a 'black, lesbian, mother, warrior, poet'. In 1982, she gave a speech called 'Learning from the 60s'.

'There is no such thing as a single-issue struggle because we do not live single-issue lives.'

Hashtag feminism

Modern feminists – sometimes referred to as fourth-wave feminists – are able to use social media to share their experiences and build communities of like-minded people.

In October 2017, actor Alyssa Milano posted a tweet calling on women to reply #MeToo if they had experienced sexual harassment or assault. The tweet went viral, and by October 2018 more than 19 million women had responded. The movement empowered women to call out unacceptable behaviour and report offenders, and highlighted how many men in power were using their positions to harass and abuse women.

▼ **SOURCE M** Alyssa Milano's October 2017 #MeToo call out, which went viral.

Alyssa Milano ✔
© Alyssa_Milano

Follow

If you've been sexually harassed or assaulted write 'me too' as a reply to this tweet.

Me too.

Suggested by a friend: "If all the women who have been sexually harassed or assaulted wrote 'Me too.' as a status, we might give people a sense of the magnitude of the problem."

1:21 PM • 15 Oct 2017

Fact ✓

The 'Me too' campaign did not begin with Alyssa Milano's tweet. It was created a decade earlier by American Tarana Burke, who wanted to help young women of colour who have survived sexual violence realise they are not alone.

▼ **INTERPRETATION N** In an introduction to a 2021 book about the #MeToo movement, Giti Chandra and Irma Erlingsdóttir – who both teach at the University of Iceland – discuss its significance.

'Is it too early to call the #MeToo movement a revolution? The initial protest seems clearly to have passed its tipping point and become a movement, but when does a movement become a revolution? If we consider the #MeToo movement as having created a platform where victims/survivors could tell their own story, a right they had been denied within the legal system or through other processes that should ensure justice, then it is possible to see the movement as a forum where anger and sorrow could be expressed in survivors' own words and be heard. This is what makes it possible, even at this early stage, to define the #MeToo movement as a revolution. [The] #MeToo movement can be called an unprecedented and historic event.'

Meanwhile...

Other online campaigns to highlight discrimination against women include the Everyday Sexism Project, a website set up in 2012 where woman can share experiences of the sexism they experience on a day-to-day basis.

The debate over the extent of progress

In October 2018, one year on from Alyssa Milano's tweet, the Fawcett Society found that 36 per cent of women and men had heard of #MeToo, and that 51 per cent of women and 58 per cent of men aged 18–34 are now more willing to challenge unacceptable behaviour.

Attitudes towards sexual harassment have, therefore, begun to change, but progress is still slow. In another survey, this time in 2021, the Fawcett Society found that at least 40 per cent of women experience sexual harassment at work and 45 per cent of women experience sexual harassment online. Women are also three and a half times more likely than men to feel unsafe walking alone after dark.

▼ **SOURCE O** Reclaim the Night is a women-only march against sexual violence and for gender equality. The first march took place in Leeds in 1977. Marches still take place in cities across Britain each year. This photograph is of the London march in 2021.

Key Words

intersectionality   gender   race   fourth-wave feminists

Meanwhile...
2018

In China in 2018, in response to #MeToo, university students came forward to share the harassment they had experienced. China has censors, who control the information shared on the internet. So, to avoid the censors, Chinese women replaced the #MeToo hashtag with two emojis: rice and bunny ('rice' is pronounced 'mi' and bunny is pronounced 'tu', so 'mi tu').

Over to You

1 In your own words, explain what 'intersectionality' means.

2 a Write a sentence or two to describe the purpose of #MeToo and a sentence or two to describe the purpose of Reclaim the Night.

   b Explain the connection between the two movements.

3 Read **Interpretation N**. Identify the reason Giti Chandra and Irma Erlingsdóttir give to explain why the #MeToo movement was a significant moment in the fight for Women's Rights.

4 What does the fact that Reclaim the Night marches still take place tell you about the fight for Women's Rights?

⟳ Quick Knowledge Quiz

Choose the correct answer from the three options.

1 Who led the National Union of Women's Suffrage Societies (NUWSS) in 1897?
- **a** Emmeline Pankhurst
- **b** Maureen Colquhoun
- **c** Millicent Fawcett

2 What was the nickname the suffragettes gave to the 1913 Prisoners (Temporary Discharge for Ill-Health) Act?
- **a** Cat and Mouse Act
- **b** Cat and Dog Act
- **c** Hunter and Prey Act

3 What was the Act of Parliament that gave all women aged 21 and over the right to vote?
- **a** Representation of the People Act
- **b** Parliament (Qualification of Women) Act
- **c** Representation of the People (Equal Franchise) Act

4 In relation to work, what happened to the majority of women when the Second World War ended?
- **a** they were relieved they no longer had to work
- **b** they left their jobs and returned to their homes
- **c** they continued with the jobs they were doing during the war

5 When was the law changed so that unmarried women could access the contraceptive pill?
- **a** 1961　　**b** 1967　　**c** 1968

6 During the Miss World protest in 1970, what did the protestors shout?
- **a** 'Deeds not words'
- **b** 'We're not beautiful. We're not ugly. We're angry!'
- **c** 'Equal pay for equal work'

7 Which Member of Parliament supported the Ford machinists' strike?
- **a** Barbara Castle
- **b** Jayaben Desai
- **c** Maureen Colquhoun

8 When was the Sex Discrimination Act passed?
- **a** 1970　　**b** 1975　　**c** 2010

9 Which term fits the definition 'the system that gives men power and largely excludes women from power'?
- **a** sexism
- **b** misogyny
- **c** patriarchy

10 What is the name of the online organisation set up in 2012 to give women the opportunity to share their experience of day-to-day sexism?
- **a** Reclaim the Night
- **b** Everyday Sexism Project
- **c** The Fawcett Society

Literacy focus

Understanding interpretations

Read Interpretation A and answer the questions below.

▼ **INTERPRETATION A** Professor Sasha Roseneil is a sociologist with an interest in gender studies. In 2020, she contributed to a book to accompany an exhibition at the British Library called 'Unfinished Business: The Fight for Women's Rights'.

> A proverb is a saying that summarises a general truth or a piece of advice that is well known. 'Necessity' means 'need' and this proverb means that if you really need to do something, you will think of ways to do it. It emphasises the idea that people are more inspired to create something when they have to, rather than when they simply want to.

'"Necessity is the mother of invention" (Old English proverb).

Women's exclusion from full and equal citizenship has given rise to a huge variety of innovative forms of protest over the last 150 years. Lacking access to the normal channels of political claims-making, women have had to find unconventional ways of articulating their demands. Working around the mainstream media's failure to grant them fair coverage, women have developed a range of creative interventions that stir the emotions, capture the imagination and disrupt everyday life. This has meant assembling unorthodox political toolkits from the resources available to them…

There have been many radically inventive moments in the history of women's struggles. These include the suffragettes, Reclaim the Night, the Greenham Common Women's Peace Camp and, recently, Sisters Uncut, who together all tell of a connected, cumulative repertoire of feminist protest. Collective occupation of public space, the direct mobilisation of women's bodies… and the use of music, song and poetry have all been distinctive methods of political engagement… Marches, rallies and demonstrations are particularly significant actions for women, who have not historically been sanctioned to gather together visibly and loudly in their own name.'

> This means the way people usually make political demands.

> 'Unconventional' means 'unusual' or 'different'.

> 'Unorthodox' means 'unusual' or 'non-traditional'.

> 'Cumulative' means 'increasing', and 'repertoire' means 'a stock of skills or methods'.

> This means to use women's bodies as a tool of protests

> 'Sanctioned' means 'given official approval'.

> 'Innovative' means 'new and creative'.

> 'Articulating' means 'clearly expressing'.

> 'Radically' means 'extreme' and 'original'.

> You have already read about the suffragettes and Reclaim the Night in this chapter. The Greenham Common Women's Peace Camp was a series of peace camps between 1981–2000 to protest against nuclear weapons being placed in Berkshire. Thousands of women spent time at the camps. Sisters Uncut fights to stop cuts to services supporting women who have experienced domestic violence. They have blocked bridges and released a colouring book.

1   Explain how women, now and in the past, have been excluded from 'full and equal' citizenship.

2   **Interpretation A** tells us that women have used innovative forms of protest.
    a   Make a list of the innovative forms of protest women have used to fight for their rights.
    b   Make a list of the more traditional forms of protest women have used to fight for their rights.

3   Professor Sasha Roseneil argues that women have had to use 'unorthodox' methods to make sure their voices are heard. Give two reasons why women have had to use unorthodox methods.

The fight for Disability Rights

Introduction

There are different ways to view and talk about disability. We have chosen to follow the definition developed by disabled people. Disability is the name for the social consequences of having an impairment. An impairment describes the way a person's body or mind is different. There are many different types of impairment: impairments are as unique as people themselves. Some you can see; some you can't. Some you are born with; some occur later in life, perhaps after an illness or an accident.

- Physical impairments describe how a person's body is different. They include medical conditions, such as epilepsy and arthritis. They also include sensory impairments, which affect a person's senses; for example, being blind or deaf.

- Mental impairments affect a person's mind, and include finding it difficult to think clearly or interact with other people; for example, having bipolar disorder. They also include learning impairments, which affect a person's ability to learn, and include finding it difficult to absorb knowledge or develop skills.

A disability occurs when the way society is organised creates barriers that prevent a person with an impairment participating fully in daily life. People have impairments, but they are disabled by society. The discrimination disabled people experience because of their impairments is called disablism.

Disabled people have always been part of society, but for many years they were often hidden from view and not granted the same rights and opportunities as other people. However, during the twentieth century disabled people increasingly started to fight for more rights, and today they are protected from discrimination by law. You are going to find out what life was like for disabled people in Britain in the early twentieth century and the different ways disabled people have fought for their rights over the years. You'll also think about what more the fight for Disability Rights has to achieve.

We are going to start with a timeline of the main events in the story of the fight for Disability Rights.

1948
Leonard Cheshire, a former RAF pilot, founds one of the best-known groups of residential care homes in the UK when he takes a dying man into his home, a country house in Hampshire called Le Court.

1958
The Brooklands Experiment shows that children with learning impairments thrive in a family environment and can be educated.

1834
The Poor Law Amendment Act is passed. People who are unable to work and support themselves are now sent to workhouses. This includes many disabled people.

1914–1918
The First World War takes place and around two million people return home to Britain with impairments.

1920
The March of the Blind takes place: 171 blind and visually impaired people travel to London to demand government support for blind and visually impaired people who cannot work. In response, the Blind Persons Act is passed in the same year.

1907
Rosa May Billinghurst, a wheelchair user, joins the suffragettes.

2015

The Independent Living Fund is closed to new applicants.

1995

The Disability Discrimination Act is passed. It requires all service providers and employers to make reasonable adjustments for disabled people.

1992

Many disabled people are infuriated by ITV's charity telethon. They feel raising money for disabled people makes them look weak and helpless. They organise the Block Telethon street party and bring an end to the telethon.

1998

The Independent Living Fund is established. Disabled people can now apply directly to the government for money to employ personal assistants.

2010

The Equality Act is passed. It replaces a range of different laws about discrimination, including the 1995 Disability Discrimination Act, with one law.

1984

The Hampshire Centre for Independent Living is set up, closely followed by the Derbyshire Centre for Independent Living. Before long, centres are established throughout England, Wales and Scotland.

1979

Project 81 is formed by a group of disabled people living at Le Court. They convince the local council to give the money being paid for their places in the residential care home directly to them. This enables them to pay for personal assistants, which in turn enables them to move out of the residential care home and into homes of their own.

1980s

The Campaign for Accessible Transport (CAT) and the Direct Action Network (DAN) are formed by disabled people to fight for, among other things, greater access to public transport.

1976

Maggie and Ken Davis move into their flat in the Grove Road Housing Scheme, which they specifically designed to enable them to live independently.

1972

The Union of the Physically Impaired Against Segregation (UPIAS) is founded by Paul Hunt.

1963

Selwyn Goldsmith writes *Designing for the Disabled*, a comprehensive guide to designing accessible facilities and buildings.

2.1 What was life like for disabled people in Britain in the early twentieth century?

In Britain, the industrial revolution made life much more difficult for disabled people, and at the beginning of the twentieth century, many were living in workhouses hidden from view. However, injured soldiers returning from the First World War, and media interest in people such as Rosa May Billinghurst, meant that disabled people were becoming increasingly visible. What was life like for disabled people at the beginning of the twentieth century? Who was Rosa May Billinghurst? And how did the March of the Blind lead to the first Act of Parliament to support disabled people?

Objectives

- Describe what life was like for disabled people in the early twentieth century.
- Explain Rosa May Billinghurst's impact on the suffragette movement and disability awareness.
- Evaluate the impact of the 1920 Blind Persons Act.

2.1A Life for disabled people in Britain in the early twentieth century

Industrial Britain

From 1700, Britain started to industrialise. For the first time, goods were made in factories rather than at home, and people moved from the countryside to find work in the growing towns and cities. Queen Elizabeth I's 1601 Poor Law had made local areas responsible for looking after people who were poor in their communities. However, tax payers argued a new approach was needed as people started to move around the country more.

In 1834, the Poor Law Amendment Act was passed. This meant that if people were unable to work and support themselves, they were sent to a workhouse. Workhouses were large buildings where people who were poor were fed, housed and given work to do to earn their keep. They were often very strictly run and people feared ending up there. Yet many disabled people had no choice: if they could not find work for themselves, they were forced into the workhouse.

Impairments were also common among people who were poor in the early twentieth century. Existing health conditions were made worse by poor-quality diets, poor-quality housing and a lack of access to medical care. Dangerous and unhealthy working conditions also meant people were easily injured. There were, therefore, lots of disabled people living in workhouses by the early twentieth century, hidden away from the general population.

▼ **SOURCE A** A photograph of women eating dinner at a workhouse in London around 1900.

Education

In the late nineteenth century, two laws established that disabled children had a right to an education, and required their parents to send them to school.

- The 1893 Elementary Education (Blind and Deaf Children) Act required school authorities to provide education for blind and deaf children.
- The 1899 Elementary Education (Defective and Epileptic Children) Act required school authorities to identify disabled children and provide them with an education.

However, the education that disabled children received was not very good; it was not like the school education children receive today. Children with physical impairments were often assumed to have learning impairments as well, and were generally trained for low-skilled work such as basket weaving. Many employers were also reluctant to give disabled people a job when they left school, even if they had gained the relevant qualifications and experience (which was very rare).

The Guild of the Brave Poor Things

In 1894, the Guild of the Brave Poor Things was set up by Grace Kimmins in London, with branches opening around the country. It set up social spaces for disabled people to meet. It also ran apprenticeship schemes for young disabled people, training them in the skills required for work. During the First World War, some employers approached Guild members to do the jobs of men who were fighting. This provided disabled people with a rare opportunity to show what they were capable of.

▼ **SOURCE B** An early twentieth-century photograph of young people wearing the Guild of the Brave Poor Things uniform.

Key Words   impairments   disability

Today, most people criticise the language the Guild used to describe impairments and disabled people. For example, its Latin motto translates as 'happy in my lot', suggesting that disabled people should not expect very much from life. In 1917, the Guild changed its name to the 'Guild of the Handicapped'. Nowadays most disabled people find the word 'handicapped' very offensive but at that time it was hoped it would encourage a more positive view of disability.

The First World War (1914–1918)

When the First World War ended in 1918, around two million people returned home to Britain with physical impairments, and carrying mental and emotional scars from their experiences. For example, it has been estimated that over 40,000 soldiers had limbs amputated during the war. Over 60,000 had serious head or eye injuries and 89,000 sustained other serious damage to their bodies. Once, disabled people were seen by some as a drain on society. Now, almost everyone knew someone with an impairment. Most respected the sacrifices the injured had made, and believed they deserved to be looked after.

A veteran is someone who used to serve in the armed forces. Houses that met the needs of disabled veterans were built, and some employers adapted their workplaces to enable disabled veterans to work and support their families. However, this increased support did not make life better for all disabled people, because it was often reserved for veterans only. The medical advances made during the First World War though did benefit many disabled people. Artificial limbs became much more widely available, for example.

Over to You

1 a What is a workhouse?
   b Why were a lot of disabled people living in workhouses at the beginning of the twentieth century?

2 a Which two laws established that disabled children had a right to an education?
   b At this time, why were many children with physical impairments trained for low-skilled work such as basket weaving?

3 Suggest one reason why the First World War might have changed many people's views about disability.

2.1B Rosa May Billinghurst: Disabled suffragette

One of the ways disabled people fight for their rights today is by demanding greater visibility. Seeing people who look like you and share the same impairments as you can be incredibly empowering. It can make you feel stronger and more confident. This is one of the reasons the story of Rosa May Billinghurst, a suffragette who used a wheelchair, is so important. At a time when most disabled people were invisible, Billinghurst was appearing on the front pages of national newspapers.

Early years

Rosa May Billinghurst was born in south London in 1875. She contracted polio when she was a child. Polio is a highly infectious disease that affects nerves in the spinal cord or brain. Billinghurst became paralysed and, unable to move her lower body, she became a wheelchair user.

▼ **SOURCE C** A photograph of Rosa May Billinghurst during a suffragette demonstration, sometime between 1908 and 1914. Her wheelchair had three wheels and was often referred to as a 'tricycle'.

Joining the suffragettes

As a young woman, Billinghurst worked with women and children living in poverty in London. She hated the unequal and unfair treatment of different groups in society, such as those in poverty (a situation known as 'social injustice'). She came to believe that if women had the vote, they would be able to make society fairer and more equal.

In 1907, Billinghurst joined the suffragettes and became involved in all aspects of their campaigning. Although not fighting for Disability Rights, Billinghurst demonstrated that disabled women had an important role to play in the fight for Women's Rights by making herself stand out in demonstrations. She decorated her wheelchair in green, white and purple, the colours of the suffragettes. She even chained her wheelchair to the railings of Buckingham Palace, alongside non-disabled suffragettes.

Connections

The suffragettes wanted to persuade the government to give women the right to vote in general elections. They used confrontational and militant (violent) campaigning methods to get as much publicity as possible for their cause.

The 'Cripple suffragette'

Billinghurst was referred to as the 'Cripple suffragette' by her fellow suffragettes and by the press. Today, referring to someone as a 'cripple' is offensive, but in the early twentieth century it was widely used to describe someone who was unable to fully use one or more of their arms or legs.

▼ **SOURCE D** An adapted extract from *The Times* newspaper, published on 13 March 1912. The 'cripple' being referred to is Rosa May Billinghurst.

'A cripple who had broken a window in Henrietta Street refused to agree to the court's conditions and was sentenced to one month's imprisonment.'

Billinghurst often used her impairment to her advantage during demonstrations.

▼ **INTERPRETATION E** Fran Abrams is a journalist and author. This is an adapted extract from a book she wrote in 2003 about the lives of the suffragettes.

'Rosa May Billinghurst was no fool. She knew full well, and so did the leaders of the suffragettes, that her hand-propelled invalid tricycle gave her a special advantage in the propaganda battle they were waging. It made it difficult, if not impossible, for the media to portray Rosa May as an angry and aggressive woman who cared little for the safety of others, which is how many suffragettes were portrayed.'

Fact ✓

Billinghurst was imprisoned several times for her part in suffragette protests. On one occasion, she refused to eat until she was released. In 1914, during one suffragette demonstration, it is said that the police deliberately tipped her out of her wheelchair. It is also said that she would hide a supply of stones under the rug that covered her knees to throw during protests.

Key Words   visibility   suffragette   social injustice   demonstration   militant

Meanwhile... 1906–1907

Rosa May Billinghurst was not the only disabled suffragette. Adelaide Knight was also a suffragette in 1906 and 1907. She used sticks to help her walk.

▼ **SOURCE F** A photograph of Adelaide Knight with her husband, Donald Adolphus Brown. They were married in 1894.

Over to You ▂▃▅

1 Why did Rosa May Billinghurst join the suffragettes?

2 a In what ways did Rosa May Billinghurst make a positive impact on the suffragette movement?

  b What can you learn from **Source D** and **Interpretation E** about the tactics Rosa May Billinghurst used to further the suffragettes' cause?

3 How did Rosa May Billinghurst increase the visibility of disabled people?

2.1C The March of the Blind

National League of the Blind

Ben Purse lost his sight at the age of 13. He trained to be a piano tuner, a skilled job that paid well. He was good at it, using his hearing to make sure that every note was exactly right. However, Purse believed he was turned down for work several times because he was blind.

Purse was fed up that blind people were prevented from earning a living because of discrimination. He wanted society to recognise the abilities of blind people. He wanted workers who were blind to have the same rights as workers who were not blind. He also wanted the government to support blind and visually impaired people who could not work, so they did not have to rely on charity. Therefore, in 1899 he decided to establish the National League of the Blind to campaign for these things. The organisation was made up of blind and visually impaired people only.

▼ **SOURCE G**
A photograph of Ben Purse in 1925.

The March of the Blind

Ben Purse and the other members of the National League of the Blind knew that if they wanted things to change, they would need to convince the government. So in April 1920, Purse and 170 blind and visually impaired people travelled from Newport in South Wales, Manchester and Leeds to London. Along the way, they carried banners saying 'For Justice Not Charity', to make sure the people they met knew what they were fighting for. The march became known as the March of the Blind.

When the marchers arrived in London they held a rally in Trafalgar Square, which was attended by 10,000 people. Five days later, a handful of the marchers, including Purse, met with the Prime Minister to explain their demands. Although they didn't achieve everything they set out to achieve, the March of the Blind put pressure on the government: later that year, the Blind Persons Act was passed. It is, therefore, an example of what activism – campaigning to bring about political or social change – can achieve.

▼ **SOURCE I** An adapted extract from an article that appeared in the *Birmingham Daily Gazette* newspaper on 26 April 1920. It describes the March of the Blind.

'With haversacks, waterbottles, and other stuff on their backs, they tramped along four abreast, bearing banners appealing for "Direct Government Support" and "No Charity", to the tunes of marching songs, the playing of bugles, and the shrill notes of the pipes of the various bands of ex-Service men who accompanied them.'

▼ **SOURCE J** David Lawley was a former miner who was blinded by a dynamite explosion in 1913. He belonged to the National League of the Blind and helped to organise the march.

'Of 35,000 blind people in the country 20,000 were existing below the poverty line. There were 850 beggars on the streets of London and 200 at Manchester. The blind have lost faith in charitable institutions being able to promote their welfare, and what they wanted was state aid to make the unfortunate class, to which they belonged, as self supporting as possible.'

► **SOURCE H**
A photograph, taken in 1920, of the March of the Blind.

▼ **INTERPRETATION K** Keith Valentine leads the Royal National Institute of Blind People (RNIB). In 2020 he spoke to the BBC to mark the 100 year anniversary of the March of the Blind.

'The march is symbolic of what's possible if you take the action yourself. It's the sense of "this is not fair, and I will not be pushed around, and I am a citizen of this country."'

Fact ✓

Two of the first official organisations to represent the rights of disabled people were formed in the late 1800s: the National Association for the Deaf and Dumb (1886) and the British Deaf and Dumb Association (1890). The word 'Dumb' is an outdated and offensive term that was used to describe a deaf person who does not communicate through speech.

Later on... 1936

Another march that attempted to highlight social injustice took place in October 1936 when 200 unemployed men marched from Jarrow, in the north east of England, to London. They wanted to draw the government's attention to the unemployment and poverty being experienced in the town.

The Blind Persons Act

In August 1920, the government passed Britain's first disability-specific legislation: the Blind Persons Act. It led to improvements for blind and visually impaired workers. For example, a pension is a regular payment made by the government to people who are over a specific age. The Act reduced the pension age of blind and visually impaired workers from 70 to 50, allowing them to stop working earlier.

The Act also required local authorities to provide services for blind and visually impaired people, including workshops and places for them to live.

However, local authorities responded differently to the Act, which meant the experiences of blind or visually impaired people were very different depending on which part of the country they were in. The Act also failed to establish a minimum wage for blind and visually impaired people. Nevertheless, it was an important moment in the fight for Disability Rights in modern Britain.

▼ **INTERPRETATION L** In 1928, Ben Purse wrote a book called *The British Blind: A Revolution in Thought and Action*. In this adapted extract, he talks about the impact of the Blind Persons Act on blind and visually impaired people.

'The 1920 Blind Persons Act gave a blind person the opportunity to win themselves a place in society by the exercise of their own initiative and capacity.'

Over to You .ıll

1   Look at the following dates. Each one is important in understanding Ben Purse's contribution to the fight for Disability Rights: August 1920, 1899, April 1920.

   a   Write out the dates in chronological order.

   b   Next to each date, write out what happened and how it is important for understanding Ben Purse's contribution to the fight for Disability Rights.

2   Like many blind people in the early twentieth century, Ben Purse found it difficult to get work. Explain why.

3   Copy and complete the following table about the 1920 Blind Persons Act.

Ways in which the Act improved the lives of blind and visually impaired workers	Ways in which the Act failed to improve the lives of blind and visually impaired workers

Interpretation Analysis

How convincing is **Interpretation L** about the impact of the 1920 Blind Persons Act? Explain your answer using **Interpretation L** and your contextual knowledge.

2.2 How have disabled people fought to live independent lives?

When most people talk about 'living independently' they usually mean that they do things for themselves and have the freedom to make their own decisions about how they live. Being able to live independently as adults is something most of us take for granted. But this has not always been the case for disabled people. By the middle of the twentieth century, many disabled people lived away from non-disabled people and were prevented from making their own choices. Where were a lot of disabled people living in the mid-twentieth century? What does 'independent living' mean for a disabled person? And how have disabled people fought to live independently?

Objectives

- Investigate where many disabled people lived in the mid-twentieth century.
- Explore what the medical model and the social model of disability meant for independent living.
- Examine the early years of the UK's Independent Living Movement.

2.2A Living in institutions

An institution is an organisation that is founded for a particular purpose. For example, a school is an institution founded to educate young people, and a hospital is an institution founded to care for the sick. Although today most people interact with institutions all the time, very few actually live in them. This was not the case for disabled people living in Britain in the middle of the twentieth century. It has been estimated that, by the second half of the twentieth century, tens of thousands of disabled people lived in institutions, separated from non-disabled people.

▼ **SOURCE A** Baroness Wilkins, a former Member of Parliament (MP), speaking in the House of Lords in 2006.

'When I first became disabled in the mid-1960s, the only prospects for people who needed help with their personal care were to be looked after by their families, to marry their nurse, or to end up in residential care.'

Colonies

In the late 1800s and early 1900s, there was increased popularity in the idea that people with learning impairments should be kept apart from those without learning impairments. As a result, in the years after the First World War (1914–1918), lots of new settlements were built across Britain to provide permanent homes for children and adults with learning impairments. To many, they were known as 'colonies'.

Connections

When one group of people are kept apart from another group of people, they are segregated from them. In the 1950s, in the southern states of the USA, white and Black people were often segregated within society. Segregated spaces included schools, libraries and cinemas.

There were often up to 1,000 people in each colony, living in large houses. Men, women and children lived separately, with up to 60 people sleeping in large dormitories in each house. If they were able to, they worked without pay on small farms, laundries, workshops or stables within the colony grounds. Some people had their own cooking and washing facilities. Children had their own schools, where they learned the basic life skills needed to live as adults in the colony. However, despite a level of independent living for some, the colonies were little more than work camps.

During the Second World War (1939–1945), some people left the colonies to work in factories and others went to fight. After the war, the colonies continued to operate and some stayed open into the 1990s.

Long-stay hospitals

Some disabled people, particularly those with physical impairments, lived in long-stay hospitals such as the Mary Dendy Hospital in Cheshire and the Caterham Asylum in Surrey. Like the colonies, these institutions were designed to keep disabled people separate from non-disabled people.

Some young people spent their entire childhoods living in hospitals. Sometimes they were placed with older people who were dying. Often, disabled young people would campaign hard to be moved to a different type of institution with a greater degree of independence. However, there were very few of these places, so many lived their entire lives in hospital.

▼ **INTERPRETATION B** Michele Gilbert reflects on her experience living in a long-stay hospital in an article published in *The Guardian* newspaper in 1966.

'At the age of 16 in 1943, I entered a geriatric [older people] ward. There was nowhere else for me it seemed... for 23 years the geriatric ward of the Chronic Hospital has been home to me. I was told on arrival that as I couldn't walk, I would have to stay in bed permanently. The days were monotonous, the routine unvarying and the rules and regulations in their number and inhumanity might have been devised for an institution for the punishment of criminals.'

Residential care homes: a new type of home

In the 1950s, there was an increasing belief that disabled young people should not live in long-stay hospitals. Several charities began to build residential care homes and one of the best known is called Leonard Cheshire.

In 1948, a former RAF pilot named Leonard Cheshire took a dying man (who had nowhere else to go) into his home, a country house in Hampshire called Le Court. The two men became friends and soon several other people with complex needs, illnesses and impairments asked Cheshire for help. By 1950, his home had 24 residents. By 1955 there were five Leonard Cheshire Homes in Britain and by 1970 there were 50.

Residential care homes offered the people who lived there a greater level of independence than in long-stay hospitals, but they were still institutions. Residents had to follow the rules and sometimes slept in large

rooms full of beds, so there was very little privacy and no place to entertain friends. Also, the homes were often in the countryside, so transport links were poor, leading to a greater sense of isolation.

Paul Hunt

Paul Hunt spent his teenage years living in a long-stay hospital and in 1956, at the age of 19, he fought hard to be moved to Le Court. While at Le Court, he and other residents began to campaign for greater independence.

Hunt's ideas and writings from this period were hugely influential on the fight for Disability Rights. In 1972, he founded the Union of the Physically Impaired Against Segregation (UPIAS). The organisation's work inspired the development of both the social model of disability and the Independent Living Movement (see pages 38 and 39).

▼ **SOURCE C** A photograph of Paul Hunt (right) at Le Court in 1964.

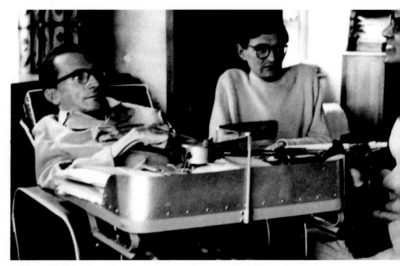

Over to You

1 In relation to disability living, what is an institution?

2 For each of the following, explain what they were and why a disabled person might not like living there:

 a colonies   c residential care homes

 b long-stay hospitals

3 What do you think is meant by the term 'independent living'? Write a definition.

2.2B Defining 'independence'

By the 1950s and 1960s, many thousands of disabled people were living in institutions. These differed from town to town and county to county, but one thing was constant: most disabled people had very little (if any) choice about where or how they lived. And some were not happy about it: they wanted to live more independent lives.

Living independently

When disabled people talk about living independently, it means they want the ability to choose, control and direct the way they live their lives. It doesn't mean they don't want any help. Few of us live truly independent lives; we all have help. We eat food grown by other people, use electricity generated by other people and ask for help from other people when our gadgets break. Rather, living independently means disabled people want to be able to choose the type of help they receive and when they receive it. They want to have the same opportunities to make decisions about their lives as non-disabled people, and they want to be able to fully participate in society.

Exactly what independence means varies from person to person, and this is as true for disabled people as it is for non-disabled people. For example, a person with a physical impairment will be able to make more decisions for themselves than someone with a mental impairment, and a person with a mental impairment may be able to carry out more personal-care tasks without support than someone with a physical impairment.

The social model versus the medical model

The idea of living independently flows directly from the social model of disability. This way of viewing disability was developed by disabled people to better describe what being disabled means. The social model of disability is very different from the medical model of disability, which is the way many people used to view disability and the way some people – including some charities and the government – still do.

The medical model of disability focuses on what disabled people *cannot* do. This way of thinking about disability looks at impairments as conditions that are 'wrong' and in need of 'fixing'. In contrast, the social model of disability shifts the focus from the individual to society.

In the social model of disability, a person is disabled because of the way society is organised. If society changes and becomes more inclusive – if the barriers that prevent disabled people participating fully in daily life are removed – disabled people can live independent lives just the same as non-disabled people. In other words, if society is better organised, it will *enable* people rather than *disable* them.

▼ **SOURCE D** A cartoon showing the barriers that prevent disabled people from taking a full and equal part in society. Attitude barriers are about views of disability, physical barriers are about how transport and buildings and so on are designed, and organisational barriers are about how parts of society are organised in such a way as to exclude disabled people.

▼ **INTERPRETATION E** The charity Disability Nottinghamshire has the following examples of the social model of disability on its website.

'A wheelchair user wants to get into a building with a step at the entrance. Under a social model solution, a ramp would be added to the entrance so that the wheelchair user is free to go into the building immediately. Using the medical model, there are very few solutions to help wheelchair users to climb stairs, which excludes them from many essential and leisure activities.

A child with a visual impairment wants to read the latest best-selling book to chat about with their sighted friends. Under the medical model, there are very few solutions but a social model solution ensures full text audio-recordings are available when the book is first published. This means children with visual impairments can join in with cultural activities on an equal basis with everyone else.'

Changing times

Although the social model of disability wasn't developed until the 1970s and 1980s, disabled people first began to think about the ideas that would lead to its development in the 1950s and 1960s. Some people living in institutions began to challenge the way these places were run. They felt neglected and forgotten, and looked for ways to gain greater control over their own lives. These were the first stirrings of the Independent Living Movement.

▼ **SOURCE F** A 1959 photograph of Albert Baker, a resident at Le Court. He was unable to use his hands so painted using a brush in his teeth.

Key Words

social model   medical model
Independent Living Movement

Meanwhile...

Parents and families established campaigning organisations to improve the lives of disabled people. For example, in 1946 the National Association for Mental Health, and the National Association of Parents of Backward Children were formed. These later became MIND (offering information and advice to people with mental health challenges) and Mencap (working with people with learning impairments). Many other organisations followed.

Over to You

1   In your own words, describe the difference between the social model of disability and the medical model of disability.

2   a   Look at **Source D**. Write down as many different barriers as you can think of that disabled people face.

    b   Colour-code each barrier you have written down using three colours: one for attitude barriers, one for physical barriers and one for organisational barriers.

    c   Which type of barrier do you think has the biggest impact on disabled people? Explain your answer.

3   Look at **Interpretation E**. How are these examples of the social model of disability?

4   On page 37 you were asked to write a definition of the term 'independent living'. Does it need changing? Rewrite it if you think it could be improved.

2.2C The Independent Living Movement

In the 1970s, some disabled people living in institutions began to explore ways to leave these places and live more independent lives. Their experiences led to what became known as the Independent Living Movement. This was a social movement that fought for disabled people to gain the freedom to have the same choices that non-disabled people have in housing, transportation, education, employment and so on.

American inspiration

In the late 1960s in the USA, a small group of disabled students, led by Ed Roberts at the University of California, Berkeley, successfully campaigned to make the whole university accessible to all. This led to the creation of the first Centre for Independent Living in 1972. One of the Centre's key aims was to fight for changes that would give disabled people access to community life, education, transport, employment and so on.

One of the Centre's first successes was to persuade the city of Berkeley to help wheelchair users by lowering some of the city's high pavement edges (known as 'curb cuts' in the USA and 'dropped kerbs' in the UK). The US Centre for Independent Living would soon inspire disabled people in the UK.

Fact ✓

The 'curb cut effect' is the phenomenon of features that are disability-friendly being used and appreciated by different groups of people. For example, curb cuts (or dropped kerbs) were first made for wheelchair access but are now enjoyed by many others as an easy way to ride a bike, skateboard or push a pushchair onto the pavement. Another example is subtitles for television programmes and films: originally designed to help deaf people, subtitles are now enjoyed by non-deaf people too.

Grove Road Housing Scheme

Maggie and Ken Davis were told, over and over again, that they had to live in an institution. They disagreed! In 1972, they began work on a purpose-built property which was specifically designed to enable them to live independently.

The Grove Road Housing Scheme in Nottinghamshire contained five flats: three ground-floor flats for disabled people and two first-floor flats for non-disabled people (employed to support the disabled residents). The Davis' worked closely with the design team to make sure that the building met their needs. For example, the kitchen sink and work surfaces were lowered, and special equipment called hoists allowed them to move to and from their bed and bathroom to their wheelchairs.

▼ **SOURCE G** Maggie and Ken Davis moved into their own home on 13 September 1976. In this 1983 photograph, they are in their living room at the Grove Road Housing Scheme.

Project 81

In 1979, a group of disabled people living in Le Court, a residential care home in Hampshire, formed Project 81. They chose the name because 1981 was to be the United Nations' International Year of Disabled Persons. The project leaders, including Philip Mason, John Evans, Philip Scott, Tad Polkowski and Liz Briggs, wanted disabled people to make decisions about their lives for themselves so that they could have more control over what happened to them.

Project 81 negotiated with the local council, convincing the council to give the money that was being provided to pay for their places in the residential care home directly to them. This enabled them to pay for personal assistants, which in turn enabled them to move out of the residential care home into their own homes in the community.

▼ **INTERPRETATION H** John Evans, one of the founders of Project 81, writing about the Independent Living Movement in 2003.

'At the same time when the "Project 81" Group were attempting to come to a negotiated settlement to enable them to live independently in the community, they also embarked upon an intensive exploration of what other disabled people were doing around the UK. They discovered that there were other groups of disabled people with similar aspirations and ideals, around the importance of developing the Independent Living ideas and philosophy, in order to empower and transform the lives of disabled people in the UK.'

Hampshire Centre for Independent Living (HCIL)

In 1984, the Hampshire Centre for Independent Living was set up. It was the first of its kind in the UK. It was run by disabled people and supported all disabled people irrespective of their impairment, gender, sexual orientation, age, ethnicity or background.

Among other things, the centre provided support, advice and information about direct payments. A direct payment is money given directly to a disabled person, rather than to the organisations or individuals caring for them. When a disabled person receives direct payments, they are able to choose and pay for exactly the right kind of support to suit their personal circumstances. For example, they can decide to pay for a personal assistant to help at work, or to live independently if they want to.

The HCIL was closely followed by the Derbyshire Centre for Independent Living. Before long, Independent Living centres were established throughout England, Wales and Scotland.

Key Words   gender   sexual orientation

Funding issues

In 1998, the Independent Living Fund was established in Britain. For the first time, disabled people could apply directly to the government for money to employ personal assistants. This was a huge milestone in the fight for Disability Rights. However, many of the barriers that prevent disabled people from taking a full and equal part in society continue to exist.

One of the barriers that has been particularly difficult to overcome is the issue of funding. The money disabled people need to lead independent lives is often under threat. For example, the Independent Living Fund was closed to new applicants in 2015, and the payments disabled people receive are rarely in line with the increasing cost of living.

▼ **SOURCE I** In 2014, Disabled People Against Cuts (DPAC) organised a protest against the proposed plan to close the Independent Living Fund to new applicants.

Over to You

1 Why was the work of a small group of disabled students at the University of California, Berkeley important for Britain's Independent Living Movement?

2 Describe the work of each of the following:
   a Maggie and Ken Davis
   b Project 81
   c Hampshire Centre for Independent Living

Knowledge and Understanding

Describe the role of the Independent Living Movement?

How have disabled people fought for equality?

Throughout the twentieth century, disabled people fought for their right to participate fully in society and to have the same opportunities as non-disabled people. Spurred on by the development of the social model of disability, disabled people have campaigned for equal access to buildings and to public transport, for equal access to appropriate educational opportunities, and to be treated with respect not pity. What barriers do disabled people face? How have disabled people fought for equality in education? And how successful have they been in changing attitudes towards charity?

Objectives

- Describe how disabled people have fought for equal access to buildings and public transport.
- Outline how educational opportunities for disabled children have changed.
- Examine what many disabled people feel about charity.

2.3A Access to buildings and public transport

The social model of disability shifts the focus from individuals to society: people are disabled because of the way society is organised and not by their impairments. If buildings and public transport are designed with disabled people in mind, they *enable* rather than *disable* people to live active, fulfilling lives. This seems logical and fair, but the people who design our towns and cities and run our public transport systems haven't always thought this way (and sometimes still forget about the needs of disabled people).

Designing for disabled people

In the decades after the Second World War (1939–1945), Britain's towns and cities grew rapidly. But it was difficult – nearly impossible – for disabled people to work and participate fully in society when Britain's buildings and urban areas were a complex maze of narrow roads, tight stairways, high kerbs, awkward entrances and exits and unaccommodating transport systems.

In 1956, a newly qualified architect named Selwyn Goldsmith contracted polio (a highly infectious disease that affects nerves in the spinal cord or brain) and became paralysed. As a new wheelchair user, he quickly identified that buildings contained many barriers that prevented disabled people from using them. Working with the Polio Research Fund and the Royal Institute of British Architects, he wrote a book called *Designing for the Disabled* in 1963. It became a comprehensive guide to designing accessible facilities and buildings. This was an entirely new concept at the time and the book is still used by architects today.

▶ ▼ **SOURCE A** Before mobile phones, if you wanted to make a telephone call while you were out, you used a telephone box. The first photograph shows a traditional telephone box. The second photograph shows a disabled-access telephone box. Both photographs were taken in 1991.

In 1964, Goldsmith moved to Norwich and used the city to further his research into disabled access. He interviewed 284 disabled people and asked them what features of buildings and facilities made life particularly difficult for them. Public toilets were top of the list, but restaurants, shops, churches and pavement kerbs were also mentioned. Because of his research, a new disabled-access public toilet was opened in the city and 15 dropped kerbs were installed on the streets around Norwich.

Design for all

In the 1970s and 1980s, there were some changes to the way new buildings were designed. In some cases, instead of adding features to help disabled people *after* a building was completed, accessibility features were incorporated into the initial design. In 1976, for example, newly built Hove Town Hall in West Sussex won a disabled access award for its entrance, and in 2004, new features made the Tower of London far more accessible. However, progress is very slow, and despite the principles of 'design for all', many disabled people still struggle to access buildings, facilities and public transport in all parts of the UK.

CAT and DAN

In the late 1980s, two organisations took the fight for Disability Rights to the streets. The Campaign for Accessible Transport (CAT) focused on one of the most challenging physical barriers: access to public transport, in particular buses. If disabled people, particularly wheelchair users, cannot board buses then their ability to travel is severely limited. This makes it extremely difficult for them to do things that non-disabled people take for granted, like getting to work, going shopping and spending time with friends.

The Direct Action Network (DAN) also demonstrated against inaccessible public transport and buildings. It was common to see members of DAN blocking bus lanes and chaining themselves to trains and other public spaces that excluded disabled people.

Both CAT and DAN campaigners carried out many demonstrations and protests from the late 1980s onwards.

▼ **SOURCE B** Wheelchair users from DAN campaigning against inaccessible buses on Westminster Bridge in London in 1995.

Meanwhile... 1981

The United Nations declared 1981 the International Year of Disabled Persons. This recognised the growing number of disabled people fighting for their rights around the world. What was happening in Britain in the 1980s and 1990s was, therefore, part of a global movement.

Over to You

1 Who was Selwyn Goldsmith and why was he an important figure in the fight for equal access for disabled people?

2 Who, or what, were CAT and DAN?

Source Analysis

1 Describe what you can see in **Source B**.

2 Give two things you can infer from **Source B** about the fight for accessible transport in the 1980s and 1990s. Describe what you can infer and provide details from the source to support your description.

2.3B Equal access to appropriate educational opportunities

In the early twentieth century, young people with impairments were considered incapable of being educated. Many spent their whole lives living separately from people who were non-disabled. Disabled children were commonly sent to live in institutions and learned only basic skills and crafts.

This system also meant that disabled young people rarely had the opportunity to interact with, or develop friendships with, non-disabled young people. This could leave disabled children feeling isolated and devalued. Also, denying non-disabled young people the chance to have disabled friends sometimes led them to develop the incorrect view that disabled people were 'different' and 'outsiders'.

Changing education policy

During the Second World War (1939–1945), many reformers and politicians thought hard about the sort of Britain they wanted to see after the conflict was over. They felt that the sacrifices people were making should result in a better future. Consequently, towards the end of the war (and in the few years after it) lots of changes took place. For example, the National Health Service (NHS) was introduced, and pensions for the elderly were increased. Education also changed. The 1944 Education Act raised the school leaving age from 14 to 15 in order to give children a longer education. The Act also recognised that mainstream schools were the best place for disabled children to be educated. For example, schools were asked to buy adapted furniture to support disabled children.

The 1944 Education Act also recognised that it was not always possible to educate a disabled child within a mainstream school, so 11 types of special school – each focusing on a different group of impairments – were created. The number of pupils attending special schools increased from around 38,000 in 1945 to nearly 107,000 in 1972, suggesting that, despite the Act, many disabled children were not given the opportunity to attend a mainstream school. Furthermore, some disabled children were still categorised as 'ineducable' (incapable of being educated) so were left without any schooling at all.

Meanwhile... 1958

In 1958, the Brooklands Experiment compared the progress of children with learning impairments who lived in hospitals, with the progress of children with learning impairments who lived in a family environment. The children in the family environment were taught using the same techniques used in nurseries attended by children without learning impairments. After two years, the children in the family environment were able to communicate and interact more. These results showed that children with learning impairments thrived in a home environment and could be educated.

▼ **INTERPRETATION C** Jane Campbell was diagnosed with Spinal Muscular Atrophy (a genetic condition that makes the muscles weaker over time) in 1959. Although she did not have a learning impairment and she desperately wanted to learn, Campbell was sent to a special school. In this adapted extract from a 2020 interview, she talks about the experience.

'I was an angry rebel when I was ten. I was very aware of my exclusion and lack of academic learning, even at that age. All we did was weave baskets and endless, needless physiotherapy. I was bored out of my mind repeating "why aren't I doing the same as my sister?"'

Fact ✓

In 2007, Jane Campbell became Baroness Campbell of Surbiton and joined the House of Lords. She is one of the very few disabled people in Parliament. Only five MPs are open about having a disability. However, if the number of disabled MPs reflected the number of disabled people in Britain, there would be 136.

More changes

Following growing pressure, the 1970 Education (Handicapped Children) Act finally removed the 'ineducable' category, meaning that all disabled children were to receive an education. Then, following the 1981 Education Act, disabled children were for the first time recognised as individuals with individual needs. They were no longer referred to by the outdated and generalised term 'handicapped'. Instead, each child with special educational needs was assessed and a written statement of their requirements prepared. The Act stated that, wherever possible, these needs should be met in a mainstream school but, if this was not possible, the child should be able to attend a special school.

Two systems

The two school systems – mainstream schools and special schools – still exist in Britain. Today, over 1.5 million school-age children are recognised as having special educational needs. Around 90 per cent of these children are educated in mainstream primary or secondary schools, while the other 10 per cent attend a special school.

Having equal access to appropriate educational opportunities means that each disabled child is able to go to a school that enables them to learn and to fulfil their potential. For some this will mean attending a special school that has specialist staff and facilities, and for some this will mean attending a mainstream school where they will be provided with additional support. Unfortunately, there are a limited number of special school places so not everyone who wants to go to one will get in. Similarly, while some disabled children thrive in a mainstream school, not all mainstream schools are set up to fully support all disabled children.

▼ **INTERPRETATION D** Zara was born in 1985 in London. She attended a special school initially, then transferred to a mainstream primary school at the age of seven. In this adapted extract, she talks about continuing with mainstream education at secondary level. She later went on to university.

'I wasn't allowed to go out at break times because they found it difficult to get me up and down stairs. They discouraged me from taking part in any of the activities that involved going off site, so I wasn't allowed to learn to swim with my classmates or go on any trips. They really didn't know quite what to do with me and didn't enjoy my presence in the school. They would wait until I was out of classes to tell my classmates about opportunities like trips abroad or opportunities to be involved in school plays. They actively didn't want me involved in anything.'

▼ **INTERPRETATION E** Mark was born in 1960, and his story features on a website of interviews with disabled people about their school experiences.

'At the time I was walking on crutches... And they organised a trip to Cleethorpes Zoo, which was about 50 km away, as a school trip out. And the school decided that I couldn't go because he [Mr Freake] couldn't look after me and take care of the other children. So this would be like 1967, and Mr Freake, my wonderful hero that he is now, said that if he didn't take me, then the whole class weren't going, which was incredible when you think back at that time. And what he did, he borrowed his grandma's wheelchair and took me. But from my memory we never used that, I was on his shoulders most of the day.'

Over to You

1 Where did the 1944 Education Act recognise was the best place for disabled children to be educated?

2 Write a paragraph of no more than 35 words to describe the difference between a mainstream school and a special school.

3 a Look at **Interpretation C**. What type of school did Jane Campbell attend?

   b What does **Interpretation C** tell you about the success of the 1944 Education Act?

4 Write sentences of no more than 30 words on each of the following:

   a The Brooklands Experiment

   b The two-tier education system

2.3C 'Nothing about us without us'

During the nineteenth century, wealthy people and religious organisations set up lots of charities that aimed to help people they viewed as vulnerable and in need. This included people who were poor, orphans and also disabled people. For example, the Guild of the Brave Poor Things was established in 1894. It set up social spaces for disabled people to meet, and ran apprenticeship schemes for disabled young people. Today, there are many charities that aim to help disabled people.

However, many disabled people reject the idea of charity because they think it reinforces the belief that disabled people should be pitied and are in need of rescue, and this belief undermines their independence. In the 1990s, the slogan 'Nothing about us without us' became popular among disabled activists, who wanted people to understand that decisions that have an impact on disabled people must be made *by* disabled people or *with* disabled people.

Later on... 2003

In 2003, DAN held demonstrations outside the offices of four big disability charities, including Scope and Mencap. It wanted to draw attention to the fact that the charities speak for disabled people but are not run by disabled people. They also accused the charities of supporting policies that did not provide real choice, independence and dignity for disabled people.

Block Telethon

In 1988, ITV organised a 24-hour charity telethon to raise money for disabled people. However, it infuriated many disabled people, who felt it made them look weak and helpless in order to raise money. When ITV broadcast a second telethon in 1990 and a third in 1992, two disabled activists – Barbara Lisicki and Alan Holdsworth – decided to organise a protest. The 1992 Block Telethon street party blocked the road outside ITV's studios and ITV finally got the message. It did not broadcast a fourth telethon!

▼ **SOURCE F** Alan Holdsworth was interviewed by *The Independent* newspaper in 1992. He organised Block Telethon with Barbara Lisicki.

'It portrays us as tragic, pathetic victims who long to be non-disabled, or plucky heroes who deserve a pat on the head for triumphing over adversity. Well, we've had enough of it.'

▼ **INTERPRETATION G** Barbara Lisicki organised Block Telethon with Alan Holdsworth. In 2018, she wrote an article about the 1992 protest called 'Block Telethon 1992 – the day we 'pissed on pity'.'

'It was a display of collective rage by disabled people, angry at the broadcast media for stealing our image and our dignity. And it was also a party, a celebration, a gathering of up to two thousand disabled people and our supporters showing that we were proud, angry and strong.'

▶ **SOURCE H** A photograph of Block Telethon protestors outside ITV's studios in 1992.

► **SOURCE I**
Disabled people protested at the annual BBC Children in Need fundraising events in the 1990s too. This leaflet was given out in 1993.

CHILDREN IN NEED (...OF WHAT ?)

RIGHTS NOT CHARITY

IT DOESN'T HELP AND IT DOESN'T CHANGE THE WAY DISABLED PEOPLE ARE TREATED

When you go home tonight and turn on the television you will be watching Children in Need and thinking how good it is to help the needy ?

You might be surprised to learn that 1000's of disabled people up and down the country will not be watching but will be there in person, demonstrating their anger at this spectacle of pity and humiliation.

As disabled people we are sick and tired of the way we are portrayed by such charity events which claim to work on our behalf but neither represent, consult or benefit us.

As disabled people, including disabled children, what we need are **RIGHTS NOT CHARITY** ...

> The **RIGHT** to use public transport.
> The **RIGHT** to gain employment.
> The **RIGHT** to get into public buildings.
> The **RIGHT** to the housing we want.

In fact, the complete right to be treated as an equal member of society - not an object of pity !

The Disability Discrimination Act

In 1970, the Chronically Sick and Disabled Persons Act was passed. It required local government to provide a range of services for disabled people, including practical assistance for people living in their own homes and access to leisure and educational facilities. Yet, the Act did not protect disabled people from discrimination. The Sex Discrimination Act of 1975 and the Race Relations Act of 1976 made discrimination on the basis of sex and race illegal, but disabled people did not have the same rights.

However, disabled people's activism led the government to pass the Disability Discrimination Act in 1995. For the first time, all service providers and employers were required by law to make reasonable adjustments for disabled people. Critics argued that there were problems with the new law: it defined disability very tightly so people with an impairment that fell outside the definition were not protected. Nevertheless, it was a turning point in the fight for Disability Rights.

Equality Act

In 2010, the Equality Act replaced a range of different laws about discrimination, including the 1995 Disability Discrimination Act. This new law was designed to make it much easier to understand what was illegal and how you could take action if you felt you had been discriminated against. It aimed to ensure that disabled people were protected from discrimination in education, work and many other aspects of daily life.

Connections

The range of different laws replaced by the 2010 Equality Act included the 1975 Sex Discrimination Act and the 1976 Race Relations Act. The Act also made it illegal to discriminate against people because of their sexual orientation or their gender reassignment for the first time.

There's still a long way to go

Disabled people have fought for and won a lot of rights, but there is still a long way to go before disabled people have the same opportunities as non-disabled people. However, we can all work together to make things better by being aware of the barriers disabled people face and being more inclusive in the way we think and act.

Over to You

1 In the 1990s, Disability Rights activists used three slogans to summarise why they were angry and what they wanted. Describe what each of the following means:

  a 'Nothing about us without us'

  b 'Piss on pity'

  c 'Rights not charity'

2 Why did Disability Rights activists object to events like ITV's 24-hour telethon and the BBC's Children in Need?

3 a Look around you and identify three barriers that prevent disabled people from taking a full and equal part in society.

  b What could a disabled person do to challenge the barriers they experience?

⟳ Quick Knowledge Quiz

Choose the correct answer from the three options.

1. Rosa May Billinghurst joined which organisation to persuade the government to give women the right to vote in general elections?
   - a   suffragists
   - b   suffragettes
   - c   Women's Movement

2. Which year was the Elementary Education (Blind and Deaf Children) Act passed?
   - a   1834   b   1859   c   1893

3. Who set up the National League of the Blind in 1899?
   - a   Ben Purse
   - b   Ben Hurst
   - c   Alan Holdsworth

4. What name was given to the new settlements built across Britain after the First World War to provide permanent homes for children and adults with learning impairments?
   - a   colonies
   - b   Leonard Cheshire Homes
   - c   workhouses

5. Who founded the Union of the Physically Impaired Against Segregation (UPIAS) in 1972?
   - a   Leonard Cheshire
   - b   Maggie Davis
   - c   Paul Hunt

6. Which model of disability focuses on society changing and becoming more inclusive?
   - a   medical model
   - b   social model
   - c   asylum model

7. The Hampshire Centre for Independent Living was the UK's first centre for independent living. When did it open?
   - a   1979   b   1981   c   1984

8. Why was CAT set up in the late 1980s?
   - a   to challenge the physical barriers disabled people experienced in accessing public transport
   - b   to campaign for all disabled people to have personal assistants
   - c   to challenge the barriers disabled people experienced if they wanted to live independently

9. Which phrase is used by disabled people to demonstrate that they want decisions that affect them to be made by disabled people?
   - a   Nothing about us without us
   - b   Children in need
   - c   Brave poor things

10. In what year was the Independent Living Fund closed to new applicants?
    - a   2010   b   2015   c   2020

Literary focus

Analysing an article

1   This extract is from a BBC article written in 2014, 20 years after the Spastics Society changed its name to Scope. Read the article carefully and answer the questions:

> The term 'spastic' was originally a medical word connected to the health of muscles. Over time it became an insult for people with cerebral palsy, which is the name for a group of lifelong conditions that affect movement and coordination. The term 'spastic' is considered extremely offensive today.

'In 1994 Blur and Oasis were slogging it out for the Britpop crown, Don't Forget Your Toothbrush was the hot TV show and people with cerebral palsy were still referred to as spastics.

Valerie Lang was on the executive council of the Spastics Society at the time. She has cerebral palsy and had been passionate about a name change for years before it eventually happened. "I felt that we could not afford to stay with the name we had," she says. "The name spastic was a playground term of abuse."

"Mothers with young babies who had cerebral palsy weren't seeking help from the society because they had heard the word used in playground parlance [everyday language]. I think it put the younger generation off."

Lang, now 74, says that people ceased to think of those with cerebral palsy as individuals. "We might have a brain injury in common but we are all different and don't want to be put in a box labelled 'spastic'."

The charity made the change at a general meeting in March 1994.

'Scope' was one of several names considered. Others were reminiscent of the single-word abstract names popular with companies in the 1990s – Clipper, Clasp, Canopy, Patch, Ibex, Cognosis, Capability. Other more traditional names under discussion included Action Cerebral Palsy and the Cerebral Palsy Society.

One of the big factors in choosing Scope, a largely neutral name with no obvious link to disability or cerebral palsy, was that it could not be turned into a term of abuse.'

a   In what year did the National Spastics Society change its name to Scope?

b   According to Valerie Lang, why did the Spastics Society decide to change its name?

c   Why, according to the article, was Scope finally chosen?

d   Other disability charities have changed names in recent years. Find another example and outline why the change occurred.

Writing in detail

2   Look at the paragraph to the right. It is a very basic answer to the question 'Define and outline some of the work of the UK's Independent Living Movement'. Rewrite the paragraph to include more details: add names, examples and facts where possible.

> The Independent Living Movement is the name given to the campaign to enable people to live more independent lives. Lots of people were involved with the campaign and there were lots of successes.

It's important to be specific. Which particular group of people are you talking about?

Can you add anything to this? What does living an independent life mean for disabled people?

This is far too general. This is where you should include examples; think about Maggie and Ken Davis, Project 81 and other groups that fought for independent living. You could also reflect on the successes of the Independent Living Movement and mention the Independent Living Fund here too.

Introduction

Often when they see the phrase 'Civil Rights', most people immediately think about the Civil Rights Movement in the USA and about Rosa Parks, Martin Luther King and Malcolm X. Few people have heard about the fight for Black Civil Rights in Britain, or have heard of Claudia Jones, Paul Stephenson and Alex Wheatle. However, Black people in Britain also fought for equal rights: to be treated the same – politically, economically and socially – as white people.

Between 1948 and 1971, nearly 500,000 people migrated to Britain from the Caribbean. The Windrush generation, as they came to be known, were not the first Black people to live in Britain. However, they faced many challenges because of their race. The term 'race' groups humans according to shared physical features, such as skin colour, hair texture and facial features. When they arrived in Britain, members of the Windrush generation were treated differently because of the way they looked, and they had to fight to receive the same opportunities and freedoms as white people.

You are going to explore what life was like for Caribbean migrants when they arrived in Britain and how a race riot in Notting Hill in 1958 led to the biggest celebration of Caribbean culture in Britain. You are also going to find out how a group of Black men in Bristol started the British Civil Rights Movement in 1963, and explore the causes and consequences of the violence that took place in Brixton in 1981. Along the way, there will be time to reflect on what more needs to be done to eliminate racial inequality.

We are going to start with a timeline of the main events in the story of the fight for Black Civil Rights.

1959
The first Caribbean Carnival takes place at St Pancras Town Hall in London.

1948
A ship carrying migrants from the Caribbean, the *Empire Windrush*, docks in Tilbury, London.

1958
Claudia Jones sets up the *West Indian Gazette*, Britain's first major Black newspaper, in London.

Race riots take place in Notting Hill in London and in Nottingham, after young white men attack Black men.

1963
Inspired by the Montgomery Bus Boycott in the USA, the West Indian Development Council in Bristol organises the Bristol Bus Boycott.

1948
The British Nationality Act is passed. People living in countries throughout the British Empire and the Commonwealth are given the opportunity to become British citizens, and with that the right to live and work in Britain.

1993
Stephen Lawrence is murdered in a racially motivated attack.

1987
Three Black MPs are elected: Diane Abbott, Bernie Grant and Paul Boateng.

1999
The Macpherson Report into the police's handling of the murder of Stephen Lawrence is published. It publicly acknowledges, for the first time, that the Metropolitan Police Service (London's police force) is institutionally racist.

1985
Cherry Groce is shot and permanently paralysed by police, triggering two days of violence in Brixton. A few days later, Cynthia Jarrett dies of heart failure when police raid her home, triggering violence in Tottenham in London.

1981
Thirteen young Black people are killed in a house fire in New Cross in London. A fourteenth person dies later as a result of the trauma.

Police launch Operation Swamp 81, triggering three days of violence in Brixton in London.

The Scarman Report into the violence in Brixton is published. It states that the violence was a spontaneous response to the resentment that had developed because of the police's use of the Sus Law.

1966
The Notting Hill Street Festival becomes the first Notting Hill Carnival when a Trinidadian steel band starts walking through the streets.

1976
The third Race Relations Act is passed, establishing the Commission for Racial Equality to enforce the first two Race Relations Acts.

1968
MP Enoch Powell makes a speech that becomes known as the 'Rivers of Blood' speech. It illustrates the growing hostility to immigration in Britain.

The second Race Relations Act is passed, extending the ban on racial discrimination beyond public places to include, among other things, the workplace and housing.

1965
The first Race Relations Act is passed: racial discrimination is banned in public places, and it becomes illegal to promote racial hatred. Discrimination is the unjust treatment of people because they belong to a particular group; people experience discrimination for many reasons, including race, gender, gender identity, sexual orientation and disability.

Earlier on... 1500s–1900s

The Caribbean is home to a number of Indigenous peoples, including the Taíno. However, the trade in enslaved people during the fifteenth to nineteenth centuries meant that thousands of people from Africa were forcefully migrated to the Caribbean. Therefore, many people from the Caribbean have ancestors who originally came from Africa.

3.1 What does the Notting Hill Carnival reveal about Britain's Caribbean community?

When the Second World War (1939–1945) came to an end, Britain was on the winning side. However, after the celebrations had died down, the reality was bleak: it would take thousands of workers to rebuild a shattered nation. People from across the British Empire and the Commonwealth were invited to move to Britain and help. Many came, particularly from the Caribbean. Yet life in Britain was far more difficult than they ever imagined. What was life like for Caribbean migrants in Britain in the 1950s? How did a race riot lead to a beautiful celebration of Caribbean culture? What is the legacy of the very first Caribbean Carnival in Britain?

Objectives

- Describe the experience of Caribbean migrants in Britain after the Second World War.
- Explain the origins of the Notting Hill Carnival.
- Analyse the legacy of the Notting Hill Carnival.

3.1A The experience of Caribbean migrants in Britain in the 1950s

Rebuilding Britain after the Second World War

After the Second World War, the government needed thousands of workers to get the country running again. Workers were needed to rebuild the towns and cities destroyed in bombing raids, and to staff newly formed organisations like London Transport and the National Health Service (NHS). In order to fill these jobs quickly, the government encouraged people from across the British Empire and the Commonwealth to move to Britain.

In July 1948, the British Nationality Act was passed. People living in countries throughout the British Empire and the Commonwealth were given the opportunity to become British citizens, and with that the right to live and work in Britain. People who took this opportunity to migrate to Britain believed they would be welcomed by the 'mother country', and would find good jobs with much higher wages. The reality, for most, would prove very different.

Empire Windrush and the Windrush generation

In May 1948, a Jamaican newspaper published an advert offering cheap tickets to anyone wanting to sail on a ship leaving shortly for Tilbury, in Britain. On arrival, the advert said, passengers would find lots of well-paid jobs, as well as places to live. Passengers on board the ship, the *Empire Windrush*, disembarked at Tilbury docks on 22 June 1948. There were 1,027 passengers on board, including hundreds from Jamaica and other parts of the Caribbean. They all arrived hoping for a better life.

It is estimated that between 1948 and 1971 nearly 500,000 people migrated to Britain from the Caribbean. They became known as the Windrush generation.

▼ **SOURCE A** A photograph of passengers on the *Empire Windrush*, which arrived in Britain in June 1948, carrying people from Jamaica and other British colonies.

Workers from Eastern Europe were also invited to Britain to fill some of the jobs available. As part of the European Voluntary Workers scheme, around 90,000 Eastern Europeans arrived in the first few years after the Second World War, mainly from Ukraine, Poland and Latvia.

Life in Britain for the Windrush generation

Life for most Caribbean migrants arriving in Britain in the late 1940s and 1950s was not what they were expecting. Despite many having highly skilled jobs in the Caribbean, working as doctors, engineers and lawyers, most were forced to take low-skilled jobs when they arrived. This was because their qualifications often weren't recognised in Britain, and because of the colour of their skin.

Many also struggled to find somewhere to live, as many white landlords refused to rent their houses to Black people. Signs saying 'No Blacks' appeared in the windows of houses with rooms to rent. As a result, Caribbean migrants were forced to find accommodation in poorer areas, where people were less reluctant to provide housing to Black people.

Thousands of white migrants also settled in Britain after the Second World War. However, hostility was more often than not reserved for Black migrants. Racism – discrimination based on a person's race – was present in every aspect of their new lives in Britain.

▼ **INTERPRETATION B** Rudy Braithwaite migrated to Britain as part of the Windrush generation. In 2019, he shared his memories of what it was like when he first arrived from the Caribbean.

'The atmosphere was bad. People would come into the corner shop and they would be served before me, you know, and I would stand there, of course too reserved [shy] to say anything about it. I remember one blonde woman with a basket in hand, she said: "These [offensive racist term] are everywhere, everywhere. I mean you can't get rid of them. Everywhere. We went through them with the war, and now we have them here, everywhere."'

migrants   race   legacy
racism   discrimination

Black Britons

Migration from Africa and the Caribbean to Britain was not new. There has been a notable Black population in Britain since Tudor times and the number increased as international trade increased and the British Empire grew. This means that when the Windrush generation started to arrive, there were around 20,000 Black people already living in Britain.

However, during the 1950s the increase in migration from the Caribbean meant Black people who had been born in Britain were less likely to be seen as Black British and more likely to be seen as migrants. This meant they shared the discrimination experienced by new arrivals.

▼ **INTERPRETATION C** In this adapted 2019 extract, Paul Stephenson shares his memories of being Black British in the 1950s.

'My grandmother was born in Britain and we, as a black family, go back about 200 years. I was born just before the war. I was well accepted. I was living in Germany when the riots broke out in Notting Hill, and when I got back to England I saw large numbers of Caribbean people arriving by train. It was the largest crowd of black people I had ever seen in my life, but it made me look and become aware of the transformation that was happening in England and that I would be seen to be an immigrant and no longer a Black English boy; and I then knew there was going to be a real challenge to Britain as to how black people were going to be received in this country.'

Over to You

1 Name two organisations that needed staff after the Second World War.

2 a Explain what Caribbean migrants expected when they arrived in Britain.

   b Explain how the experiences of Caribbean migrants when they arrived in Britain differed from their expectations.

3 Read **Interpretation C.**

   a List three things we can learn about the life of Paul Stephenson from the interpretation.

   b What does the interpretation suggest about the treatment of Black British people after the arrival of the Windrush generation?

3.1B Claudia Jones and the first Caribbean Carnival

Moving to Notting Hill

After the bombing during the Second World War, there was a severe shortage of housing in London. Many people were desperate to find somewhere to live. The houses in Notting Hill were extremely run-down, but it was cheap to rent a room in a shared house. A lot of landlords focused on making money by renting to as many people as possible: in some cases, as many as ten people slept in one room, often in shifts.

When Caribbean migrants arrived in London, Notting Hill was one of only a handful of places where landlords would rent to them. This, coupled with the cheap rents, meant many made Notting Hill their home.

Tension quickly started to build in the area, as the white working-class people living in Notting Hill felt the newly arrived Caribbean migrants were taking their homes and their jobs. Racism increased and Black people were often prevented from visiting shops and restaurants run by white people. Violent racism also grew: groups of young working-class white men – called Teddy Boys, because of the distinctive clothes they wore – became openly hostile to Black people.

Claudia Jones

Claudia Jones was born in Trinidad in the Caribbean in 1915, and moved to the USA as a young child. She worked for newspapers and openly supported calls for better working conditions and equal rights for African Americans. In 1955, she was forced to leave the USA and she was granted refugee status in Britain.

In March 1958, Jones set up Britain's first major Black newspaper, the *West Indian Gazette and Afro-Asian Caribbean News*, in Brixton in London. It brought Caribbean communities living across London together, providing a place to share information about work, housing and events. It informed readers about fights for racial equality around the world, including the work of the Civil Rights Movement in the USA. It also encouraged Black people to fight for their Civil Rights.

▼ **SOURCE D** Claudia Jones also campaigned against discrimination in housing, education and employment. She suffered a heart attack in December 1964 and died aged 49.

Notting Hill Riots

In the summer of 1958, groups of Teddy Boys began attacking the homes and businesses of Black residents in Notting Hill. On 24 August 1958, these attacks escalated into rioting. Groups of young white men first attacked five Black men with metal bars, then attacked an interracial couple (a Black Jamaican man and a white Swedish woman), and continued to target Caribbean cafes, shops and homes. Black residents took to the streets to protect themselves. The rioting that followed lasted a week before police were able to gain control.

Meanwhile... 1958

On 23 August, a race riot also broke out in Nottingham after a Black Caribbean man was seen enjoying a drink with a white British woman, and was violently attacked.

The first Caribbean Carnival

After the riots in Notting Hill and Nottingham, racial tensions remained very high. Claudia Jones and others came up with the idea of organising a Caribbean Carnival. They hoped it would give Caribbean migrants an opportunity to celebrate their shared heritage, as well as bring Caribbean culture to a wider audience. Claudia Jones said she hoped it would 'wash the taste of Notting Hill and Nottingham out of our mouths'.

In January 1959, Britain's first Caribbean Carnival was held in St Pancras Town Hall in London. It therefore became known as the London Carnival. It was shown on television by the BBC and was a huge success. A series of similar indoor events were held around London until Jones died in 1964. In 1966, the first outdoor event took place and today the Notting Hill Carnival is an annual event, attracting two million visitors each year.

▼ **SOURCE E** A photograph showing participants enjoying the first Caribbean Carnival in St Pancras Town Hall in 1959.

▼ **INTERPRETATION F** In 2019, Donald Hinds (born in the Caribbean and arrived in Britain in the 1950s) shared his memories of the origins of the Notting Hill Carnival.

'Claudia [Jones] asked for suggestions which would wash the taste of Notting Hill and Nottingham out of our mouths. It was then that someone, most likely a Trinidadian, suggested that we should have a Carnival – in winter? It was a December of 1958. Everybody laughed and then Claudia called us to order. "Why not?" she asked. "Could it not be held in a hall somewhere?"'

Key Words refugee Civil Rights

▼ **INTERPRETATION G** Chris Mullard, born in the Caribbean and lived in Britain in the 1950s, became one of the lead organisers of the Notting Hill Carnival. In 2019, he described the atmosphere in London in 1958. The British Fascist Movement was a British political group that shared similar values with the Nazi Party in Germany.

'It came out of this cauldron, if you like, of hate which was expressed by white people towards black people in the 1950s in the country. I remember walking down the street, just down here where I live... you know, being spat at, being bullied, being attacked by the British Fascist Movement, who had their offices up the end of the street.'

▼ **INTERPRETATION H** Historians Patrick Vernon and Dr Angelina Osborne remembered Claudia Jones as one of 100 Great Black Britons in 2020.

'Claudia Jones' death at the age of forty-nine ripped a hole in the fabric of Caribbean society. In the eight years she lived in England she had her finger on the pulse of British society, using her remarkable gifts to create unity and strength within the early Black British communities.'

Over to You

1 Why was the first Caribbean Carnival organised?

2 Give two reasons why racial tension was building in Notting Hill in the early 1950s.

3 Read **Interpretation H**.
   a Summarise the point the interpretation makes about the impact of Claudia Jones' death.
   b Why do you think Claudia Jones had such a significant impact on life in Britain?

4 Plaques are often put up on the outside of buildings to remember significant individuals or significant events. Write a 50-word plaque to go up on the outside of St Pancras Town Hall.

3.1C The legacy of the Caribbean Carnival

Notting Hill Carnival

After the death of Claudia Jones in 1964, many people felt there was still a need to celebrate the shared heritage of the many Black people living in Britain. In 1966, Rhaune Laslett-O'Brien organised the first outdoor event: the Notting Hill Street Festival. Lots of the performers had performed at Jones' Caribbean Carnival for many years.

During the Street Festival, a Trinidadian steel band started walking through the streets of Notting Hill, performing, dancing and celebrating Caribbean culture. And so the Notting Hill Street Festival became the first Notting Hill Carnival, with 1,000 people in attendance.

Learning about other cultures helps people become more tolerant and accepting, and the organisers hoped the Notting Hill Street Festival would give lots of people from all over London an opportunity to experience Caribbean culture. This, they believed, would help resolve some of the tensions between Black and white communities in London. The Street Festival would also give Black people an opportunity to celebrate their identities and heritage, helping them to recover when they experienced racism.

▼ **SOURCE I** A photograph of Notting Hill Carnival in the 1970s. By the 1970s, it had become the largest street festival in Europe.

St Pauls Carnival, Bristol

As well as London, many Caribbean migrants also settled in Bristol, in an area called St Pauls. There, they shared many of the same experiences as those in London: poor housing, difficulty getting work and racism.

In 1968, inspired by the Notting Hill Carnival, a street festival was held in St Pauls to celebrate Caribbean culture. It was a small community event, where local people sold home-cooked food in front of their homes and music played. Today, St Pauls Carnival attracts thousands of visitors every year.

1976 Notting Hill Riot

By 1976, the Notting Hill Carnival was a huge success, with around 150,000 people travelling to West London to attend. However, the carnival had not succeeded in ending racial tension. In fact, tension between Black people and the police in particular was getting worse. For example:

- In May 1959, a young Black man called Kelso Cochrane was murdered. Two white men were arrested but released a few hours later without being charged. Police played down the motive as robbery, refusing to listen to the local community who told them the murder was racially motivated. To this day, no one has been convicted of Cochrane's murder.

- Police regularly raided Black businesses, including a popular restaurant called the Mangrove. The local community organised a demonstration against the harassment. 150 people took part in the demonstration, which was accompanied by 200 police officers. After violent clashes, police arrested nine people, who came to be known as the Mangrove Nine. They were charged with inciting a riot, which carried a long prison sentence. They were eventually found not guilty, and the judge acknowledged the police's behaviour was motivated by racial hatred.

- The Sus Law (short for Suspected Person) gave police the power to stop, search and arrest people who they suspected were about to commit a crime, without the need for evidence or witnesses. As a result, many Black people were arrested for no reason at all and charged with 'Sus'.

In 1976, the Notting Hill Carnival ended in widespread rioting. It is believed to have started when police attempted to arrest a young Black man they suspected of being a pickpocket. Several other young Black people came to defend him and things quickly escalated. More than 100 police officers and around 60 carnival-goers were taken to hospital, and 66 people were arrested.

Connections 🔗

Other fights for rights are characterised by conflict with police. For example, in 1910 the suffragettes organised a demonstration in Parliament Square. Instead of the demonstrators being arrested, there were violent clashes and reports of women being beaten and sexually assaulted by police. The day came to be known as Black Friday.

Notting Hill Carnival today

Despite the events of 1976, Notting Hill Carnival has remained an important part of London's cultural life, and it's still the largest street festival in Europe. It is held every summer over the August bank holiday weekend and attracts over two million people every year, with over 40,000 volunteers working behind the scenes to make it happen.

▼ **SOURCE J** A photograph of Notting Hill Carnival in 2022. The carnival is still a celebration of Caribbean culture, with parades, bands, sound systems and food stalls.

Over to You 📶

1 Look at the following dates. Each one is important for understanding the legacy of the first Caribbean Carnival, organised in 1959: 1976, 1968 and 1966.

   a Write out the dates in chronological order.

   b Next to each date, write out what happened in that year and how it is important for understanding the legacy of the first Caribbean Carnival.

2 Write a short account of the 1976 Notting Hill Riots. Make sure you use the following in your answer:
   • 150,000 people
   • racial tensions
   • police
   • pickpocket
   • young Black people

Significance

1 What were the two aims of the first Caribbean Carnival, organised in 1959?

2 For each aim, describe – using examples – how far it has been fulfilled.

3 'The first Caribbean Carnival has a tremendous legacy, fulfilling the aims it set out to achieve.' How far do you agree? Explain your answer.

3.2 How successful was the Bristol Bus Boycott?

In Britain in the 1950s, it was not illegal to discriminate against people because of their race. A group in Bristol, called the West Indian Development Council, decided they needed to act. Inspired by events in the USA, the 1963 Bristol Bus Boycott kick started the British Civil Rights Movement, and led to the 1965 Race Relations Act. What triggered the Black British community to protest against discrimination in the 1960s? What was the Bristol Bus Boycott? And what impact did it have on the British Civil Rights Movement?

3.2A Bristol in the 1950s

Living in Bristol in the 1950s

In 1948, the British Nationality Act was passed, which gave people living in countries throughout the British Empire and the Commonwealth the opportunity to become British citizens, and with that the right to live and work in Britain. Many took this opportunity to move to Britain.

While many Caribbean migrants settled in London, many also settled in Bristol. In 1950, there were only 1,000 Caribbean migrants in Bristol, but by 1962 around 3,000 people from the Caribbean had settled in the city. Like Caribbean migrants in other parts of the country, they experienced racism, and so many struggled to find places to live and work because they were Black. Many ended up settling in an area called St Pauls.

Most of the houses in St Pauls were in appalling condition. Many were still damaged from the Second World War and lots were overcrowded. But it was one of the few places new arrivals could afford to live. As a result, St Pauls became known as a predominately 'Black' area, despite the fact that most of the people who lived there were white. This led to rising tensions between Bristol's white and Black residents, with Black residents wrongly blamed for the poor condition of housing in St Pauls.

The Civil Rights Movement in the USA

By the 1950s, there was a growing sense that everyone – regardless of the colour of their skin – had a right to political and social freedom, a right to equality. In the USA, the Civil Rights Movement was gaining momentum as African Americans fought against the racism and discrimination they faced on a daily basis.

> **Meanwhile...**
>
> By the 1950s, some former British colonies, such as India and Ghana, had gained their independence from the British Empire, encouraging other colonies to continue to fight for their freedom. However, a racist system called apartheid had been legally established in South Africa. It segregated (separated) the majority Black population from the white minority and gave white people far more rights than Black people.

In the 1950s, in the southern states of the USA, buses were segregated and Black passengers had to give up their seats for white passengers when the white section of a bus was full. In 1955, a Black woman named Rosa Parks was arrested when she refused to give up her seat for a white passenger. A few days later, the Montgomery Bus Boycott began. A boycott is when you stop using a service or a product as a form of protest, and the Montgomery Bus Boycott is considered to be the first full-scale campaign against segregation.

African Americans refused to ride the buses in the Alabama city of Montgomery until the bus system was desegregated (no longer separated). Eventually, after 13 months, the US Supreme Court declared segregated buses were illegal, and the boycott became an inspiration for people fighting for their Civil Rights around the world.

▼ **SOURCE A** Rosa Parks after she was arrested for refusing to give up her seat for a white passenger in 1955.

Bristol's 'colour bar'

In 1950s Britain, it was not illegal to discriminate against people because of their race. This led to the introduction of 'colour bars'. The 'colour bars' were racist policies that meant people of African, Caribbean and Asian heritage (collectively referred to as 'coloured' at the time) were denied opportunities available to white people, including access to jobs, restaurants, leisure facilities and housing. These policies were enforced by business owners, sometimes with the support of local police officers.

> ### Fact ✓
>
> 'Coloured' and 'Black' were terms used to describe African, Caribbean and Asian people until the late twentieth century. 'Coloured' is not a term commonly used anymore because it is offensive.

The Bristol Omnibus Company ran the city's buses, and in 1955 its workers voted to introduce a 'colour bar'. This meant that African, Caribbean and Asian people could not be employed as bus drivers or bus conductors. The racist policy was brought to public attention in 1961, but a manager at the company was unapologetic. He defended the 'colour bar' on the basis that white bus drivers and conductors did not want to work with African, Caribbean and Asian bus drivers and conductors, and that the they were not skilled enough.

Key Words   segregated   boycott   desegregated   'colour bars'   'coloured'

▼ **SOURCE B** Cyril Buckley worked for the Bristol Omnibus Company and this is an adapted extract from an interview he gave to the BBC in 1963.

'Well, we are as such at the present time operating a colour bar simply because, whilst we can within this city, we shall go on encouraging white labour before coloured labour. This is the policy of the company in light of the experience in other cities and towns where they have engaged the coloured labour and their labour situation has got worse.'

▼ **INTERPRETATION C** Paul Stephenson is the son of a Caribbean migrant and went on to become an important figure in the British Civil Rights Movement. In this adapted extract from 2019, he describes what living in Bristol in the 1960s was like.

'Black people had no rights. I was arrested and thrown in jail for refusing to leave a public house. Couldn't work on the buses. Couldn't be a policeman. Couldn't be a fireman.

It was a time when Martin Luther King was marching and the students down south in the USA were marching for freedom and against discrimination and racism, and I felt that something had to be done in Bristol.'

> ### Over to You 📶
>
> 1 a How many Caribbean migrants had settled in St Pauls, Bristol by 1962?
>   b Explain why many Caribbean migrants arriving in Bristol settled in St Pauls.
>
> 2 What was the Montgomery Bus Boycott?
>
> 3 Read **Interpretation C**.
>   a What does it suggest about life for Black people in Bristol in the 1960s?
>   b Paul Stephenson explains that events in the USA made him feel that something needed to be done in Bristol. Which important Civil Rights victory in the USA do you think inspired Stephenson and why?

3.2B The Bristol Bus Boycott

The West Indian Development Council

When the 'colour bar' on Bristol's buses became public knowledge in 1961, four Jamaican men living in Bristol began to campaign against it. Owen Henry, Roy Hackett, Audley Evans and Prince Brown formed the West Indian Development Council (WIDC). They were joined by Paul Stephenson, who became the group's spokesperson.

Stephenson was born in Essex in 1937. His father was West African and his mother was English. He was educated, a good speaker and very persuasive – the perfect person to challenge the negative stereotypes of Black people in Britain in the 1960s.

▼ **SOURCE D** A photograph of Paul Stephenson taken in 2005. Stephenson was Britain's first Black youth officer and he went on to become a significant Civil Rights activist.

The call to boycott

Stephenson realised the WIDC needed proof that the 'colour bar' existed: something that could be used to persuade local people to oppose the discrimination taking place at the Bristol Omnibus Company. He got a Black Jamaican, called Guy Reid-Bailey, an interview for a job as a bus conductor. Reid-Bailey was more than qualified for the job, but his application was rejected as soon as the interviewer saw that he was Black. Inspired by the Montgomery Bus Boycott, Stephenson responded by calling for a boycott of Bristol's buses.

▼ **INTERPRETATION E** In 2019, Guy Reid-Bailey recalled his attempt to get a job at the Bristol Omnibus Company in 1963, and describes the racism he experienced.

'I did apply for a job as a bus conductor and an interview was arranged for me to come to the bus station for an interview... when I actually got to the reception area, the receptionist said to the manager "Oh, Mr Bailey is here; he's black." And the manager then spoke with me and explained that he wasn't prepared to offer me an interview because if he did he would "displease his bus crew".'

The Bristol Bus Boycott began in April 1963. It was supported by students and lecturers from the University of Bristol and soon gained national and international attention. The local MP, Tony Benn, voiced his support for the boycott and condemned the Bristol Omnibus Company, but still the company refused to employ Black and Asian bus drivers and bus conductors.

The end of the 'colour bar'

On 28 August 1963, the Bristol Bus Boycott came to an end when the Bristol Omnibus Company was finally forced to end its 'colour bar'. In September 1963, the company hired its first South-Asian bus conductor, Raghbir Singh. Days later, the company also hired two men from Pakistan and two men from Jamaica.

This victory did not bring about an end to racism in Bristol, or in Britain, but it was a significant moment in British history because it marked the start of the British Civil Rights Movement. It also encouraged people like Paul Stephenson to continue to fight against racial discrimination at all levels of society.

> **Meanwhile...** 1963
>
> Across the Atlantic, Martin Luther King – a Black Civil Rights leader in the USA – delivered his famous 'I Have a Dream' speech on 28 August 1963, the same day that the Bristol Bus Boycott ended. In the speech, he called for an end to racism, and Civil Rights for all.

▼ **SOURCE F** Today, people in Bristol are proud of the role the city played in tackling racism in Britain. This mural was put up in St Pauls in 2019 to commemorate Roy Hackett's involvement in the Bristol Bus Boycott. He was one of the founding members of the WIDC. Unfortunately, the wall collapsed in 2021, but there are plans to reinstate it.

▼ **INTERPRETATION G** In 1966, a Black bus conductor reflected on the impact of the Bristol Bus Boycott.

'I think the best thing about coloured conductors working on the buses up and down the country was that it gave the ordinary Englishman the chance of meeting a black man. Ten years ago when you gave a passenger his change and ticket, besides marvelling at the fact that you actually spoke English and that you gave him the correct change, he would also grab hold of your hand and then shout to all the bus that your hands are warm. Some, of course, gave your hands a vigorous rub to see whether it was dirt which made you black. All these things sound incredible, but they are all true. So many people put their hands on my hair for good luck in the first year of my working on London buses that I was in fear of going bald prematurely.'

Over to You

1 a Who was Paul Stephenson?

   b Why was Paul Stephenson a good choice for spokesperson of the WIDC?

2 Write a short account of the Bristol Bus Boycott. Make sure you use the following in your answer:
   • West Indian Development Council
   • Paul Stephenson
   • Guy Reid-Bailey
   • August 1963
   • Raghbir Singh

3 Read **Interpretation G**. What does it suggest was one of the benefits of ending the 'colour bar' at the Bristol Omnibus Company?

3.2C The legacy of the Bristol Bus Boycott

The British Civil Rights Movement

Although many believed the Bristol Omnibus Company secretly tried to limit the number of African, Caribbean and Asian people it hired, the Bristol Bus Boycott was considered a landmark victory. Its success sparked a national movement against racial discrimination.

When we hear the phrase 'Civil Rights Movement' we often think of the USA, of Martin Luther King and Rosa Parks. However, there was also a Black Civil Rights Movement in Britain and it is a very important part of British twentieth-century history.

▼ **INTERPRETATION H** Reni Eddo-Lodge is a British journalist who wrote a book about racism in modern Britain in 2017.

'To assume that there was no civil rights movement in the UK is not just untrue, it does a disservice to our black history, leaving gaping holes where the story of progress should be.'

After the Bristol Bus Boycott, key individuals like Paul Stephenson continued to fight against 'colour bars' and discrimination against Black people. This campaigning led to new laws against racism.

The Race Relations Acts

In 1965, the **first Race Relations Act** was passed. Racial discrimination was banned in public places, and it became illegal to promote racial hatred.

In 1968, the **second Race Relations Act** was passed. This built on the 1965 Act, extending the ban on racial discrimination beyond public places to include, among other things, the workplace and housing. The government said the aim of the Act was to help integrate migrant communities, by ensuring they had fair access to jobs, housing, transport and so on.

In 1976 the **third Race Relations Act** established the Commission for Racial Equality. The Commission was tasked with encouraging better relations between people of different races, and raising public awareness of ongoing issues. It also enforced the laws created by the first two Race Relations Acts by challenging racial discrimination in the courts when it occurred. Paul Stephenson, who had played such an important role in the success of the Bristol Bus Boycott, joined the Commission.

Connections

In 2007, the Commission for Racial Equality joined with the Disability Rights Commission and the Equal Opportunities Commission to form the Equality and Human Rights Commission. Its job is to make Britain fairer by protecting people's rights.

▼ **INTERPRETATION I** Historians Patrick Vernon and Dr Angelina Osborne remembered Paul Stephenson as one of 100 Great Black Britons in 2020.

'The boycott heavily influenced the 1965 Race Relations Act, which was passed by the Labour government after meeting with Stephenson, Hackett and Bailey. It forbade discrimination on the grounds of colour, race or national origins, and was expanded three years later to include both housing and employment. In 1976 the Act was amended to include direct and indirect discrimination. Harold Wilson himself conceded that without Paul's efforts, it would have been difficult for the Labour government to introduce these laws.'

New laws

Alongside the Race Relations Acts, different British governments also introduced laws that limited migration, particularly migration from Africa, the Caribbean and Asia. The 1962 Commonwealth Immigrants Act, the 1968 Commonwealth Immigrants Act and the 1971 Immigration Act stripped away the rights given to people by the 1948 British Nationality Act. These laws made it much harder for people born in Commonwealth countries to live and work in Britain, turning them from 'British citizens' into 'immigrants': people who come to live permanently in a foreign country. These laws encouraged people who opposed immigration, and led to an increase in racial discrimination, because hostility towards immigrants is often targeted towards Black and Asian people.

Racism continues

▼ **SOURCE J** In 1968, Enoch Powell, a Member of Parliament, gave a speech which has come to be known as the 'Rivers of Blood' speech. It played an important role in making people who held anti-immigration views feel more confident.

> 'We must be mad, literally mad, as a nation to be permitting the annual flow of some 50,000 dependents... It is like watching a nation busily engaged in heaping up its own funeral pyre... As I look ahead I am filled with foreboding; like the Roman, I seem to see the "River Tiber foaming with much blood"'.

By the 1970s, a group called the National Front wanted all migrants from Africa, the Caribbean and Asia to leave Britain, and it was gaining support across the country. There was also a rise in the number of violent attacks on Black and Asian people by members of the National Front. Police did little to protect them from racist attacks and, on many occasions, abused their powers to harass young Black and Asian men. This led to violence in cities across Britain in 1981, including London, Liverpool and Birmingham.

Many groups formed to oppose the racist anti-immigration message that the National Front were spreading, including the Anti-Nazi League and Rock Against Racism. There were also protests against Enoch Powell's speech.

▼ **SOURCE K** In 1968, three weeks after the 'Rivers of Blood' speech, students from the University of Bristol gathered to protest against Enoch Powell.

Over to You

1 Look at the following dates. Each one represents an important milestone in the fight for Black Civil Rights in Britain: 1976, 1965, 1968.

   a Write out the dates in chronological order.

   b Next to each date, write out what happened in that year and how it helped the fight for Black Civil Rights in Britain.

2 Read **Source J**.

   a Describe Enoch Powell's attitude towards immigration in the 1960s.

   b Explain why the attitude of Enoch Powell and people who supported him limited the positive impact of the Race Relations Acts on the fight for Black Civil Rights in Britain.

Knowledge and Understanding

1 Which Acts of Parliament tried to improve race relations?

2 Which Acts of Parliament made relations between white British people and migrants more difficult?

3 Explain why the 1960s and the 1970s were a difficult time for race relations in Britain.

Was the violence in Brixton in 1981 a riot or an uprising?

After the Second World War (1939–1945), many migrants from the Caribbean settled in Britain to start a new life. Many found a home in Brixton in South London, where they established a vibrant Caribbean community. However, life wasn't always easy. Throughout the 1970s, Black men living in Brixton were regularly stopped, searched and arrested by police, often for no real reason at all. Then on 10 April 1981, tensions between the Black community and police erupted into violence. What caused this violence? What happened afterwards? And should the events in Brixton in 1981 be remembered as a 'riot' or an 'uprising'?

Objectives

- Identify the causes of the violence in Brixton in 1981.
- Describe the consequences of the violence in Brixton in 1981.
- Evaluate whether the violence in Brixton in 1981 should be called a 'riot' or an 'uprising'.

3.3A Brixton 1981: Causes

Moving to Brixton in the 1950s

A large number of Caribbean migrants settled in Brixton in South London. This happened almost by chance. One of the first ships bringing people from the Caribbean was the *Empire Windrush*. When it docked in London, in June 1948, a significant number of passengers were given temporary accommodation in an underground air-raid bunker in Clapham. Many then walked the short distance from Clapham to the Brixton Labour Exchange to find work.

Brixton had been badly bombed during the war, and the houses that remained were damaged and run-down. This meant rents were cheap, and many Caribbean migrants found a home in Brixton as well as work.

Meanwhile... 1950s

Many Caribbean migrants were bitterly disappointed by the discrimination they experienced in Britain. Many would have returned to the Caribbean if they could have afforded it. Also, as many Caribbean migrants had believed so passionately that Britain would be welcoming, they were ashamed to return and tell people it had not been like this for them.

▶ **SOURCE A**

A 2016 photograph of the underground air-raid bunker in Clapham where passengers from the *Empire Windrush* were housed temporarily.

Brixton in 1981

A vibrant Caribbean community

By 1981, around half a million migrants from the Caribbean had settled in Britain. Many of them moved to Brixton.

Faced with white landlords who would not rent to them and banks that required a large deposit before they would help someone buy a house, Caribbean migrants in Brixton worked together to buy their own homes. They established 'pardner' schemes. A group got together and each person contributed a sum of money on a regular basis. Every week, fortnight or month, one member of the group was given the total amount paid in over the period. This money could then be put towards a deposit for a house.

Brixton Market became famous as *the* place to buy Caribbean food, including yams, plantain and scotch bonnet chilli peppers. Caribbean restaurants opened and lovers' rock filled the airways; it was a popular British style of reggae that was melodic and romantic in style.

Recession

In the early 1980s, there was a severe economic recession in Britain – factories closed and unemployment rose. By 1981 around 10 per cent of working-age people were unemployed. With fewer opportunities to earn money by working, some people drift into crime. The recession hit Black men particularly hard. For example, in 1982 around 35 per cent of Black men of Caribbean heritage and around 15 per cent of Black men of African heritage were unemployed, compared with around 12 per cent of white men. Young Black men were increasingly blamed for the increase in crime.

A poor relationship with the police

The Black community in Brixton had a poor relationship with the police. Almost all police officers were white in the early 1980s and the Black community believed they were racist.

Dating back to the 1824 Vagrancy Act, the Sus Law (short for Suspected Person) gave police the power to stop, search and arrest people who they suspected were about to commit a crime, without the need for evidence or witnesses. As a result, many Black people were arrested for no reason at all and charged with 'Sus'.

On 18 January 1981, a house fire in New Cross in South London killed 13 young Black people (a fourteenth person died later as a result of the trauma). Many believed the fire was started deliberately, and one of a series of racist attacks against the Black community that were happening at the time. However, police quickly dismissed this line of enquiry, preferring the theory that a fight had broken out at the party and caused the fire. Police treated the survivors like suspects, and the media promoted this version of events.

In response to the New Cross fire, the Black community organised the Black People's Day of Action. On 2 March 1981, 20,000 Black people marched from New Cross to central London. The route of the march had been agreed with police in advance, but on the day police tried to stop the marchers and fights broke out. Although the demonstration was largely peaceful, the newspaper headlines described a rampaging mob.

Operation Swamp 81

On Monday 6 April 1981, police launched Operation Swamp 81. This was a massive escalation of their stop and search campaign in Brixton. In the following five days, around 1,000 people were stopped and searched.

On Friday 10 April, rumours that a young Black man had been injured during a stop and search started to circulate. A crowd gathered. Three days of violence followed: rioters, mostly young Black men, fought with police and set fire to vehicles and buildings.

▼ **SOURCE B** An extract from the lyrics to Eddy Grant's 1982 hit single 'Electric Avenue'.

'Now in the street, there is violence
And, and a lots of work to be done
No place to hang out our washing
And, and I can't blame all on the sun

Oh no, we gonna rock down to Electric Avenue
And then we'll take it higher
Oh, we gonna rock down to Electric Avenue
And then we'll take it higher

Workin' so hard like a soldier
Can't afford a thing on TV
Deep in my heart, I abhor ya
Can't get food for the kid'

Over to You

1 Why did large numbers of Caribbean migrants settle in Brixton?

2 Write one sentence to explain how each of the following helped cause the violence in Brixton in 1981:

   a a vibrant Caribbean community

   b the recession

   c the New Cross fire

   d a poor relationship with the police

3 Look at **Source B**. What can you learn from the lyrics about the problems in Brixton in 1981?

3.3B Brixton 1981: Consequences

10–12 April 1981

Between Friday 10 April and Sunday 12 April, violence raged in Brixton. 500–600 young people, mostly young Black men, expressed their frustration, resentment and anger towards the police, and the discrimination they encountered in Britain on a daily basis. There was an incredible amount of damage done: 61 private vehicles and 56 police cars were set on fire, and over 30 buildings were burned to the ground. The clashes left hundreds of police and dozens of other people injured. Around 7,000 police officers were required to establish law and order.

This violence had numerous consequences for the fight for Black Civil Rights in Britain.

Meanwhile... **1981**

The following weeks saw smaller-scale incidents occurring in Birmingham, Sheffield, Nottingham, Hull, Slough, Leeds, Bradford, Newcastle, Huddersfield, Halifax, Knaresborough, Leicester, Fleetwood, Derby, Blackpool, Wolverhampton, Maidstone, Cirencester and Luton.

The end of the Sus Law

As a result of the violence across Britain, the government decided to act. On 27 July 1981, the Criminal Attempts Act was passed. It ended the use of the Sus Law. The new law said that police could not stop and search people simply because they appeared to have done something suspicious and were hanging around. However, Black people are still almost seven times as likely as white people to be stopped and searched today.

The Scarman Report

After the events in Brixton, the government asked a judge, Lord Scarman, to investigate what had happened. The Scarman Report was published in November 1981. It concluded that Operation Swamp 81 was a 'serious mistake'. It stated that the violence had not been planned and was a spontaneous response to the resentment that had developed because of the police's methods. It also acknowledged that racism was a fact of life for Black people in Britain, and called for more Black police officers to be recruited.

However, the violence in Brixton in 1981 was not the last time conflict has erupted between police and Black communities in Britain.

- On 3 July 1981, violence erupted in Toxteth in Liverpool. The rioting lasted nine days, and was caused by the same issues experienced in Brixton: unemployment and a poor relationship between the police and the Black community.
- On 28 September 1985, Cherry Groce, a Jamaican woman, was shot and permanently paralysed by police after her Brixton home was raided. This sparked two days of rioting.
- On 5 October 1985, Cynthia Jarrett, also from Jamaica, died of heart failure when police officers raided her home on the Broadwater Farm estate in Tottenham in London. The next day, rioting broke out.
- On 4 August 2011, Mark Duggan, a British Black man, was shot by police in Tottenham in London. For five days, on 6–10 August, there were riots in cities across the country, including London, Birmingham, Liverpool and Manchester.

▼ **SOURCE C**
A photograph of Cherry Groce in 1986.

▼ **SOURCE D**
A photograph of Cynthia Jarrett in 1985.

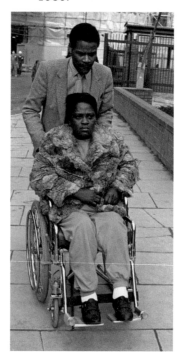

The first Black MPs

Before the violence in Brixton in 1981, there were no Black MPs in Parliament. However, in the 1987 general election, three were elected, all representing London constituencies with a large Black population.

▼ **SOURCE E**
Diane Abbott represented Hackney North and Stoke Newington.

▼ **SOURCE F**
Bernie Grant represented Tottenham.

▼ **SOURCE G**
Paul Boateng represented Brent South.

Keith Vaz, of Indian descent, was also elected to represent Leicester East. The number of Black and minority ethnic MPs has also risen in recent years, from 4 in 1987 to 65 in 2020. However, if the number of MPs from an ethnic minority background reflected the population of Britain, there would be 119.

▼ **INTERPRETATION H** Alex Wheatle is a Black British novelist who was 18 and living in Brixton during the violence in 1981.

'The events in Brixton 1981: many people see that as just plain violence. But for us, who experienced it, we saw it as standing up to a racist police force. After these events, we believe that finally society began to start listening to us and to our concerns. For the first time, Black people like myself became leaders of councils, politicians and community activists. I believe that these riots sent a stern message to government. Telling them that they can no longer treat diverse communities so badly.'

The Macpherson Report

The Scarman Report acknowledged that Black people in Britain experienced racism. However, it wasn't until the Macpherson Report was published in 1999 that it was publicly acknowledged, for the first time, that the Metropolitan Police Service (London's police force) was institutionally racist.

The Macpherson Report was commissioned by the government after Stephen Lawrence, a 19-year-old Black man, was murdered in South London in an unprovoked racist attack in 1993. During the investigation many (including the Lawrence family) felt the police were not doing enough to identify and prosecute the killers because Stephen was Black.

Acknowledging institutional racism is an important first step, but getting rid of it takes a long time. For example, in 2022, Chris Kaba, an unarmed Black man, was shot and killed by police in South London. In 2023, the Baroness Casey Review into the Metropolitan Police found they were still guilty of institutional racism and that their own officers suffer discrimination within the workplace.

Fact

Institutional racism is a form of racism that is firmly and deeply rooted in the laws and culture of a country or an organisation. It was defined in the Macpherson Report as, 'The collective failure of an organisation to provide an appropriate and professional service to people because of their colour, culture or ethnic origin.'

Over to You

1 Write a sentence or two to explain each of the following:
   a the Scarman Report (1981)
   b the 1987 general election
   c the Macpherson Report (1999)

2 Write a short news article explaining the consequences of the violence in Brixton in 1981 for the fight for Black Civil Rights in modern Britain.

Cause and Consequence

1 There are three main consequences of the violence in Brixton in 1981: the end of the Sus Law, the Scarman Report and the 1987 general election. Rank these consequences in order, with the consequence that had the biggest impact on Black British Civil Rights at the top and the consequence that had the smallest impact at the bottom.

2 'Of all the consequences of the violence in Brixton in 1981, the most important by far was the election of three Black MPs in 1987.' How far do you agree? Explain your answer.

3.3C Brixton 1981: Riot or uprising?

The violence in Brixton in 1981 is referred to as both a 'riot' and an 'uprising'. A riot is a violent public disorder; it is something negative that occurs when a group of people decide to push violently against law and order. An uprising, on the other hand, is an act of resistance; it occurs when a group of people resist injustice.

To police, politicians and the media at the time, the 1981 Brixton Riots were an example of young Black criminals committing violence and destroying things because they knew no better. To many of the people involved and to people who lived locally, the 1981 Brixton Uprising was a rebellion by young Black men who could no longer bear the racism they experienced at the hands of the police. It was the only way they had to show the depth of their pain, anger and frustration.

Whether you view the violence in Brixton in 1981 as a riot or an uprising will depend on your understanding of the history of Black Civil Rights in Britain, and on the sources and interpretations you look at.

▼ **SOURCE I** A photograph taken at the time of the violence in Brixton in April 1981. Photographs like this would have appeared on the front covers of national newspapers alongside headlines like 'Police vow: We won't be moved, then burning and looting mobs storm back on to the streets'.

▼ **INTERPRETATION J**

Jasmine Pierre is a volunteer researcher with the Museum of London's Listening to London project. In March 2022, she listened to the museum's recordings of people talking about the violence in Brixton.

'In the context of the Listening to London project, I explored the Museum of London's "Brixton Riots" collection which was recorded in 2009. When I started working with the collection, I immediately recognised that the use of the term "riot" in its title was problematic. It implies that the 1981 Brixton uprising was intentionally aggressive and unreasonable when, many would argue, it was inevitable and even a fundamentally necessary response to the injustices suffered by Black and Brown communities in London.'

▼ **INTERPRETATION K**
Alex Wheatle is a Black British novelist who was 18 and living in Brixton during the violence in 1981. Here, in an interview in the Museum of London archive, he recalls why he joined in.

'There was a bit of pride too, that we stood up for ourselves. And we were glad that we kind of said to the police enough is enough... We're gonna fight back, we're gonna fight back violently. You cannot just take liberties and come to us and do what you like with us; we're actually going to resist. There was pride in that.'

▼ **SOURCE L** An extract from a television news interview with Prime Minister Margaret Thatcher on 13 April 1981. Brixton is in the London Borough of Lambeth.

'Interviewer: But there's no trust with the police, it appears, at the moment in Lambeth. I mean somebody said today that the police in Lambeth were behaving like an army of occupation.

Prime Minister: What absolute nonsense and what an appalling remark and I condemn the person who made it. Had there been any question of the police withdrawing from Lambeth as they had temporarily to withdraw from Bristol they would have been subject to the gravest criticism. They would have been totally wrong. The job of the police is to protect the citizens. And they did protect the citizens in Lambeth to the very best of their ability and they were absolutely right to do so. No-one must condone violence, no-one must condone the disgraceful events that took place in Lambeth. They should not have happened. They were criminal.'

▼ **SOURCE M** An extract from a *Daily Telegraph* article published on 13 April 1981.

'Rioting, looting and arson spread through the rubble-strewn streets of Brixton last night in the area's second successive night of widespread violence. Police with riot shields struggled to contain the marauding gangs of youths - most, but not all of them, black. Police buses and vans were attacked and shops wrecked. At least two private cars were set on fire.
After eight hours of violence, sporadic outbreaks still continued in streets littered with shattered glass. Groups of youths pelted the police with bricks, beer cans and lumps of concrete. Firemen were attacked as they fought the flames of violence.'

Key Words riot uprising decriminalised gay bisexual

▼ **INTERPRETATION N** Ros Griffiths was 15 in 1981. She witnessed the violence in Brixton and, in 2021, reflected on her experience.

'As I got into the area, you could see the fighting. It looked like war... It was a watershed moment for race relations. I had the confidence to say enough is enough, I'm not having it. You will not call me these racial slurs, you will not refer to me as if I'm inadequate.'

Connections

The 1967 Sexual Offences Act had **decriminalised** consensual sexual relationships between men aged 21 and over. However, public displays of affection between men could still result in criminal prosecution. As a result, **gay** and **bisexual** men were also targeted by police using the Sus Law. Many white gay and bisexual men joined the 1981 Brixton Uprising to support Brixton's Black community.

Over to You

1 a In your own words, describe a 'riot'.
   b In your own words, describe an 'uprising'.

2 Look at the sources and interpretations on these pages and divide them into two categories: those that suggest the violence in Brixton in 1981 was a riot, and those that suggest it was an uprising.

3 a Look at the sources and interpretations that suggest what happened was a riot. Do they come from similar people and places?
   b Look at the sources and interpretations that suggest what happened was an uprising. Do they come from similar people and places?
   c What can you learn from the sources and interpretations about the importance of power in the way history is constructed?

⟳ Quick Knowledge Quiz

Choose the correct answer from the three options:

1 Why did the government encourage people from across the British Empire and the Commonwealth to move to Britain after the Second World War?

   a to help rebuild Britain
   b to help Britain deal with the problem of unemployment
   c to provide an opportunity for a better life

2 In what year was the British Nationality Act passed?

   a 1945   **b** 1948   **c** 1950

3 Where was the first Caribbean Carnival held in 1959?

   a St Pauls, Bristol
   b Notting Hill, London
   c St Pancras Town Hall, London

4 What event in the USA inspired the Bristol Bus Boycott?

   a Montgomery Bus Boycott
   b Notting Hill Riots
   c Martin Luther King's famous 'I Have a Dream' speech

5 What did the Bristol Bus Boycott aim to end?

   a the 'colour bar' on Bristol's buses
   b all segregation in Britain
   c an end to racist and sexist attitudes

6 Which local MP supported the Bristol Bus Boycott?

   a Enoch Powell
   b Tony Benn
   c Harold Wilson

7 Who made the speech that has come to be known as the 'Rivers of Blood' speech, which illustrated the growing hostility to immigration in Britain?

   a Enoch Powell
   b Tony Benn
   c Harold Wilson

8 When did widespread violence break out in Brixton for the first time?

   a 1993   **b** 1985   **c** 1981

9 Which one of the following was not a cause of the widespread violence that broke out in Brixton?

   a the recession
   b the death of Cynthia Jarrett
   c the police's use of the Sus Law

10 Which of the following publicly acknowledged that the Metropolitan Police Service was institutionally racist for the first time?

   a Baroness Casey Review
   b Scarman Report
   c Macpherson Report

Literary focus

Note-taking

Note-taking is a vital skill. To do it successfully, you must identify the key words and phrases in each paragraph. These are words that are vital to the meaning (and your understanding).

Look at these paragraphs:

> After the Second World War, the government needed thousands of workers to get the country running again. Workers were needed to rebuild the towns and cities destroyed in bombing raids, and to staff newly formed organisations like London Transport and the National Health Service (NHS). In order to fill these jobs quickly, the government encouraged people from across the British Empire and the Commonwealth to move to Britain.
>
> In July 1948, the British Nationality Act was passed. People living in countries throughout the British Empire and the Commonwealth were given the opportunity to become British citizens, and with that the right to live permanently and work in Britain. People who took this opportunity to migrate to Britain believed they would be welcomed by the 'mother country', and would find good jobs with much higher wages. The reality, for most, would prove very different.

The important words and phrases are: After Second World War; workers needed; government encouraged people from Brit. Empire and Commonwealth to move to Britain; 1948 British Nationality Act; become Brit. citizens; migrate to Brit.; believed welcomed; good jobs; reality different.

The original paragraphs were 142 words long. In comparison, the notes are 34 words long and contain abbreviations. Note-taking like this will help your understanding of events, and it's good practice for revision too.

1   Write down the key words and phrases from the following paragraphs. These will be your notes.

a   In May 1948, a Jamaican newspaper published an advert offering cheap tickets to anyone wanting to sail on a ship leaving shortly for Tilbury, in Britain. On arrival, the advert said, passengers would find lots of well-paid jobs, as well as places to live. Passengers on board the ship, the *Empire Windrush*, disembarked at Tilbury docks on 22 June 1948. There were 1,027 passengers on board, including hundreds from Jamaica and other parts of the Caribbean. They all arrived hoping for a better life. It is estimated that between 1948 and 1971, nearly 500,000 people migrated to Britain from the Caribbean. They became known as the Windrush generation.

b   A large number of Caribbean migrants settled in Brixton in South London. This happened almost by chance. One of the first ships bringing people from the Caribbean was the *Empire Windrush*. When it docked in London in June 1948, a significant number of passengers were given temporary accommodation in an underground air-raid bunker in Clapham. Many then walked the short distance from Clapham to the Brixton Labour Exchange to find work. Brixton had been badly bombed during the war, and the houses that remained were damaged and run-down. This meant rents were cheap, and many Caribbean migrants found a home in Brixton as well as work.

c   In 1950s Britain, it was not illegal to discriminate against people because of their race. This led to the introduction of 'colour bars'. 'Colour bars' were racist policies that meant people of African, Caribbean and Asian heritage (collectively referred to as 'coloured' at the time) were denied opportunities available to white people, including access to jobs, restaurants, leisure facilities and housing. These policies were enforced by business owners, sometimes with the support of local police officers.

The fight for LGBTQ+ Rights

Introduction

The acronym LGBTQ+ stands for Lesbian, Gay, Bisexual, Transgender, Queer or Questioning, with the + representing the wide variety of other sexual orientations and gender identities. Sexual orientation and gender identity are different but, although they present unique challenges, LGBTQ+ people have consistently been on the receiving end of similar discrimination. Discrimination is the unjust treatment of people because they belong to a particular group; people experience discrimination for many reasons, including race, gender, gender identity, sexual orientation and disability.

In Britain in the 1950s, LGBTQ+ people had to keep their true identities and their personal lives secret. Homosexual acts were illegal and society frowned upon relationships between women, and on people whose gender identities did not match the sex they were assigned at birth. In sharp contrast, today same-sex couples can marry, LGBTQ+ characters regularly appear in television shows and there are a large variety of LGBTQ+ role models. Yet, these changes did not happen automatically. LGBTQ+ people had to fight every step of the way. You are going to find out how the lives of LGBTQ+ people improved in the 1960s, how progress took a step backwards when prejudice and intolerance increased in the 1980s, and how the lives of LGBTQ+ people have been transformed in recent years. You'll also think about what more the fight for LGBTQ+ Rights has to achieve.

We are going to start with a timeline of the main events in the story of the fight for LGBTQ+ Rights.

What does it mean?

The history of the fight for LGBTQ+ Rights uses lots of key terms. You may know what some or all of them mean, but here is a reminder of some of the main ones.

- **heterosexual:** a person who has romantic and/or sexual relationships with people of a different gender
- **homosexual:** a person who has romantic and/or sexual relationships with people of the same gender; it's an outdated term and 'gay' is more generally used today
- **gender:** often expressed as male or female; gender is largely constructed by society and is assumed from the sex assigned at birth
- **lesbian:** a woman who has romantic and/or sexual relationships with women
- **gay:** a man who has romantic and/or sexual relationships with men; also a modern term for homosexual
- **bisexual:** a person who has romantic and/or sexual relationships with people of the same gender and people of a different gender
- **transgender:** a person whose gender is not the same as, or does not sit comfortably with, the sex they were assigned at birth
- **queer:** a term used by people who do not want to use a specific label to describe who they do or do not have romantic and/or sexual relationships with, and/or do not want to use traditional terms to describe their gender identity; some LGBTQ+ people think the word is insulting, but others embrace it
- **sexual orientation:** an umbrella term that describes who a person is sexually or romantically attracted to

The language used to describe sexual orientation and gender identity is constantly changing. These definitions are up to date at the time of writing, but may change over time. If you're ever in doubt about the right words to use, just ask!

1952
Home Secretary David Maxwell Fyfe openly states, in the House of Commons, that homosexuals are 'a danger to others'.

1957
The Wolfenden Report is published. It recommends that homosexual acts taking place in private between consenting adults over the age of 21 should be decriminalised (no longer treated as illegal).

1958
The Homosexual Law Reform Society is established to campaign for the decriminalisation of sexual relationships between men.

2013
The Marriage (Same Sex Couples) Act is passed. Same-sex couples can now marry in the same way as mixed-sex couples.

2021
A survey finds that 64 per cent of LGBTQ+ people have experienced anti-LGBTQ+ violence and abuse.

2004
The Civil Partnership Act is passed. Same-sex couples can now register a civil partnership, giving them virtually the same rights and responsibilities as a mixed-sex marriage.

2004
The Gender Recognition Act is passed. For the first time, transgender people can apply to change the sex recorded on their birth certificate, from male to female or from female to male.

2000 and 2003
Section 28 is removed first in Scotland and then in England and Wales.

1999
The Admiral Duncan (an LGBTQ+ pub in London) is targeted by a nail bomb in a homophobic attack.

1989
17 million people watch the first gay kiss on prime-time British television, between Colin and Guido in EastEnders.

1984–1985
Lesbians and Gays Support the Miners (LGSM) is established, forming a bond between LGBTQ+ people and striking miners, which leads to a ground-breaking vote at the Labour Party Conference to support lesbian and gay rights.

1988
Section 28 of the Local Government Act is passed, making it difficult, if not impossible, for schools to discuss LGBTQ+ issues.

1969
The Stonewall Uprising occurs in the USA. After the police raid a gay bar in New York City, hundreds of LGBTQ+ people take to the streets. This influences events in Britain.

1981
A new illness – AIDS – is found in some gay men. John Eaddie is the first recorded person to die of an AIDS-related illness in the UK. Gay and bisexual men are terrified, and discrimination against LGBTQ+ people increases.

1972
The GLF organises the first Pride march in London. 2,000 people take part.

london 1971   10p

gay liberation front **manifesto**

1967
The Sexual Offences Act is passed. Consensual sexual relationships between men aged 21 and over are decriminalised, so long as they take place in private.

1970
The Gay Liberation Front (GLF) is founded in Britain. It aims to change society and make life in Britain better for LGBTQ+ people.

4.1 Parliament, protest or pop culture: which did most to improve the lives of LGBTQ+ people in Britain in the 1950s and 1960s?

In 1950s Britain, LGBTQ+ people could not express their identities or share their love publicly. Gay and bisexual men risked prosecution and prison if police discovered their relationships, while lesbians, bisexual women and transgender men and women also tried to keep their identities and personal lives secret because society disapproved. But by the end of the 1960s, a lot had changed. What was life like for LGBTQ+ people in the 1950s? Why was the Wolfenden Report important? How did LGBTQ+ people respond to the prejudice they faced? And did the social and sexual freedoms of the 1960s improve the lives of LGBTQ+ people in Britain?

Objectives

- Outline the lives of LGBTQ+ people in the 1950s.
- Describe how attitudes towards LGBTQ+ people began to change in the late 1950s and early 1960s.
- Explain the impact of the 'Swinging Sixties' and the Sexual Offences Act on the lives of LGBTQ+ people.

4.1A Life for LGBTQ+ people in the 1950s

In 1950s Britain, most LGBTQ+ people lived very secret lives.

The vast majority of people supported heterosexual relationships and traditional gender roles: men were expected to have romantic and sexual relationships with women and to work and support their families, and women were expected to have romantic and sexual relationships with men and to stay at home and look after their husbands and children.

Society considered homosexuality a 'disease' which needed to be treated, either chemically to reduce a person's desire for a relationship with someone of the same gender, or with therapy to 'change' how a person expressed themselves romantically and sexually. Sexual relationships between men were illegal. There were no laws about sexual relationships between women (except in the armed forces), or about transgender people, but it was very hard to live openly.

The political establishment was also prejudiced. In 1952, Home Secretary David Maxwell Fyfe openly stated in the House of Commons that homosexuals were 'a danger to others'. While he was in charge of crime and policing, the number of gay and bisexual men prosecuted for homosexuality increased dramatically, from 956 in 1938 to nearly 4,000 in 1952.

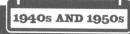

Meanwhile... 1940s AND 1950s

After a series of operations between 1946 and 1949, Michael Dillon became the first person to undergo female to male gender affirming surgery in Britain. In 1951, Roberta Cowell became the first person in Britain to undergo male to female gender affirming surgery.

Alan Turing

Alan Turing was a brilliant mathematician and computer pioneer. During the Second World War, he worked at Bletchley Park in Buckinghamshire and played a central role in building an early type of computer that could decode encrypted enemy orders. It is estimated that this work shortened the war by two to four years, saving millions of lives.

Turing was gay, and in 1952, after reporting a burglary at his home, he was arrested and convicted for being in a gay relationship. He avoided prison by agreeing to take female hormones, which were thought to reduce his desire for relationships with men. He found the side effects deeply unpleasant and, when he died in 1954, the coroner ruled that he had taken his own life.

▼ **SOURCE A** In 2013, Alan Turing was pardoned for the crime he was accused of. Then in 2021, his life and work were celebrated on the new £50 note with his image on the back.

▼ **SOURCE B** The Gateways club in London was the best-known lesbian club in Britain. This photograph was taken in about 1953.

The Montagu Case

In 1954, three men – Lord Montagu, Peter Wildeblood and Michael Pitt-Rivers – were convicted and sentenced to between 12 and 18 months in prison for having sexual relationships with other men. The public was fascinated by the trial, which was discussed in all the newspapers. But instead of abusing the three men, the crowd waiting outside the courtroom cheered. On his release from prison, Wildeblood, a journalist, wrote a book about his experiences, which was widely read. The Montagu Case was a clear sign that public opinion was changing, and that the public was no longer completely supportive of the idea of criminalising people for gay relationships.

Polari and Gateways

Despite the hostile environment they experienced, LGBTQ+ people found subtle ways to express themselves and find like-minded people to socialise with.

Polari is a language that has been around for hundreds of years, but it was used by gay and bisexual men in the 1950s to communicate with each other. This was a form of protest against discrimination. They used Polari words mixed in with English words so that most people didn't understand what they were talking about.

Flowers were also used as a form of communication. Green carnations have been worn by gay and bisexual men since Oscar Wilde, the Irish playwright who was imprisoned for taking part in homosexual acts, wore one in the 1890s. Violets have been used by lesbians and bisexual women to identify themselves as far back as Ancient Greece.

By the 1950s, there were also a handful of places where LGBTQ+ people could meet and express themselves openly; places like the City of Quebec pub and the Gateways club in London, and the New Union pub in Manchester. While there was always a risk of a police raid, these venues thrived.

Over to You

1 Give three examples that show how LGBTQ+ people were treated unfairly in the 1950s.

2 Here are some Polari words and their English translations:

bona: good	bungery: pub
buvare: drink	cove: friend
dolly: pretty	doss: bed
eek: face	fruit: gay man
gelt: money	lilly: police
naff: bad	

Work out the meaning of this sentence: 'I met my cove for a buvare in the bungery yesterday, but the lilly arrived which was really naff.'

3 Look at **Source A**. Explain what the Bank of England's decision to release a new £50 note featuring Alan Turing tells us about how the position of LGBTQ+ people in British society has changed since the 1950s.

4.1B Attitudes begin to change... slowly

In the late 1950s and early 1960s, the government's attitude towards LGBTQ+ people showed signs of changing, and LGBTQ+ people began to create support networks and protest against the discrimination they were facing. However, sexual relationships between men were still illegal and there was still a considerable sense of disgrace associated with being LGBTQ+.

The Wolfenden Report

In 1954, the government established a committee to evaluate the criminal law relating to sex, including homosexuality. John Wolfenden was chosen to lead the committee of 15 members, which included academics, judges, doctors and members of the Church of England.

Over the next three years, the committee met 62 times and heard from more than 200 organisations and individuals. The final report was published in September 1957 and recommended that homosexual acts taking place in private between consenting adults over the age of 21 should be decriminalised.

The report was a landmark moment in the fight for LGBTQ+ Rights. However, it would be a further ten years before any legal changes took place.

▼ **SOURCE C** Allan Horsfall, who founded the North-Western Homosexual Law Reform Committee, said he was 'delighted to see what the (Wolfenden) Committee had recommended'.

The Minorities Research Group

Although clubs like Gateways existed, life for many lesbian and bisexual women in 1960s Britain was very lonely. Cynthia Reid was determined to change this. As a lesbian, she felt isolated from wider society. She also felt isolated from the lesbian community because she didn't fall into one of the two roles typically expected of lesbian women: she was neither butch (dressing and behaving in a manner stereotypically associated with men) nor femme (dressing and behaving in a manner stereotypically associated with women).

Reid saw that there was a need for spaces for lesbian and bisexual women to meet, relax and talk. So, with the help of four friends, she set up the Minorities Research Group in 1963. The group met monthly in different pubs and published a magazine called *Arena Three*, which provided information, offered counselling advice and enabled lesbian and bisexual women to contact each other. The magazine provided a lifeline for lesbian and bisexual women who could not travel to the meetings.

▼ **INTERPRETATION D** An adapted extract from a 2019 interview with Cynthia Reid. Here she talks about why she set up the Minorities Research Group.

'After my relationship ended, I realised I had no one else and no means of meeting anyone else. Whereas other people could go to discos or dances, or hobby groups or whatever, and meet partners and say "would you like to come out for a coffee", you know, you can tell people you fancy them and you'd like to get to know them better and if you're a homosexual, there's no sort of group that you could go to.'

▼ **SOURCE E** A photograph of two 1966 editions of the *Arena Three* magazine.

The Homosexual Law Reform Society

Reid knew people from the Homosexual Law Reform Society, which had been set up in 1958 to campaign for the decriminalisation of sexual relationships between men. Reid's Minorities Research Group had a strong social element to it, but socialising at Homosexual Law Reform Society meetings was strictly forbidden. Members were afraid they would be arrested, despite the fact that many of them were not themselves gay.

The Society worked closely with sympathetic Members of Parliament and had many high-profile supporters, including former Prime Minister Clement Attlee. They acted as a **pressure group**, trying to change the law on homosexual relationships.

Earlier on...   1946

COC Netherlands was established in 1946, and it is the world's oldest operating LGBTQ+ organisation (COC translates as 'Centre for Culture and Leisure'). It influenced the Homosexual Law Reform Society and the North-Western Homosexual Law Reform Committee.

The Beaumont Society

Although there were no laws about transgender people, the sense of disgrace was strong enough to prevent many transgender people from being open about their identities. They were afraid of blackmail (people demanding money from them to keep their identities secret), as well as physical and emotional abuse. The Beaumont Society, which started in 1965, was a support group run by and for transgender people and their families, and it still exists today.

The Society began to produce a newsletter, the *Beaumont Bulletin*, in 1968. It provided help and guidance, as well as a contact system so that transgender people could meet each other. By 1973 there were over 200 members.

April Ashley

April Ashley was a model and actor. She attended fashionable parties, was written about in newspapers, and modelled for famous photographers. However, in 1961 the *Sunday People* newspaper published an article announcing that Ashley had received male to female gender affirming surgery in Morocco (in North Africa) the previous year. As a result, she found it difficult to get work in Britain and had to move abroad.

After her marriage failed in 1966, Ashley's ex-husband took her to court to annul their marriage. He argued that the marriage never legally happened because she was a man. The judge agreed, stating that she 'was at all times a male' and that marriage between two men was illegal.

Key Words

decriminalised   pressure group

▼ **SOURCE F** A photograph of April Ashley receiving an MBE in 2012, for services to transgender equality.

Over to You

1 a What was the Wolfenden Report?

   b Why was the publication of the Wolfenden Report an important moment in the fight for LGBTQ+ Rights?

2 Look at **Interpretation D**. Why do you think Cynthia Reid set up the Minorities Research Group?

3 Identify one similarity between the Minorities Research Group, the Homosexual Law Reform Society and the Beaumont Society, and one way in which they were different.

4 Create a poster to advertise the Minorities Research Group, the Homosexual Law Reform Society or the Beaumont Society, making it clear how the organisation you choose helps LGBTQ+ people.

4.1C Life for LGBTQ+ people in 1960s Britain

The 'Swinging Sixties'

In 1966, the American magazine *Time* described London as 'The Swinging City', recognising the new pop culture that was introducing social and sexual freedoms for some young people. Part of this was a noticeable increase in the visibility of LGBTQ+ people, and a general softening of negative attitudes towards LGBTQ+ people.

▼ **SOURCE G** An advert for the 1961 film *Victim*. This was one of the first films to have a gay man as the central character.

Meanwhile...

1960s

The 'Swinging Sixties' was a time when some young people, particularly those living in London, experimented with fashion, music, illegal drugs and new ways of living. Bands like The Beatles and the Rolling Stones were riding high in the charts. From 1961, the contraceptive pill meant women could choose whether or not they wanted to have a baby.

The 1968 film *The Killing of Sister George* was the first British film to have lesbians as the central characters. Some scenes were filmed at the lesbian club Gateways. Artists like Francis Bacon and David Hockney were openly gay, and the actor Kenneth Williams used Polari on *Round the Horne*, one of the most popular radio shows of the time. Even the *Daily Telegraph*, considered one of the most conservative newspapers in the country, argued for the abolition of laws against homosexuality.

The 1967 Sexual Offences Act

The Sexual Offences Act was passed in 1967. Following the recommendations of the 1957 Wolfenden Report, consensual sexual relationships between men aged 21 and over were decriminalised, so long as they took place in private.

This was certainly progress, but the age of consent for sex between men was still higher than the age at which a man and a woman could legally have a sexual relationship (which was set at 16 in England, Wales and Scotland, and 17 in Northern Ireland). Furthermore, gay and bisexual men were still prosecuted: there were 420 convictions for gross indecency in 1966 compared to 1,711 in 1974.

▼ **SOURCE H** An extract from an article written by Peter Tatchell, a gay rights activist. It was published in *The Guardian* newspaper in May 2017. Public order and breach of the peace laws give police a wide range of powers to prevent public disturbances.

'There were police stake-outs in parks and toilets, sometimes using "pretty police" as bait to lure gay men to commit sex offences. Gay saunas were raided… Gay and bisexual men, and some lesbians, continued to be arrested until the 1990s for public displays of affection, such as kissing and cuddling, under public order and breach of the peace laws.'

Later on...

2001

In 2001, the age of consent for sex between men was reduced to 16 in England, Wales and Scotland, and 17 in Northern Ireland, bringing it in line with the age of consent for sex between men and women.

Meanwhile...

One of the most significant acts of protest by LGBTQ+ people took place in the USA. On 28 June 1969, after the police raided the Stonewall Inn, a gay bar in New York City, hundreds of LGBTQ+ people took to the streets and fought back for six days. The events at Stonewall reverberated around the world and became an iconic moment of LGBTQ+ resistance against police brutality, and oppression.

▼ **SOURCE I** A photograph of the Stonewall Inn taken in 2019, 50 years after the Stonewall **Uprising**. You can read the detail of the commemorative plaque that sits on the front of the building.

▼ **INTERPRETATION J** In an adapted extract from a 2018 article for the BBC's History Extra website, Historian Dr Florence Sutcliffe-Braithwaite considers the significance of the 1967 Sexual Offences Act.

'The 1967 Sexual Offences Act was a hugely important moment in the history of homosexuality in Britain. But it wasn't a moment of sudden liberation for gay men, and nor was it intended to be. It had huge consequences though: in the end, it allowed the development of a more extreme and powerful gay activism. This was a key factor in pushing society's attitudes towards homosexuality to slowly change.'

Over to You

1 a When were consensual sexual relationships between men decriminalised in Britain?

 b Why was decriminalising consensual sexual relationships between men an important event?

 c Why were some LGBTQ+ people disappointed with the Sexual Offences Act?

2 Look at pages 74–79 and identify examples of how each of the following improved the lives of LGBTQ+ people in Britain in the 1950s and 1960s:

 a Parliament

 b protest

 c pop culture

Significance

1 Which of the following did most to improve the lives of LGBTQ+ people in Britain in the 1950s and 1960s: Parliament, protest or pop culture? Discuss with a partner and then rank them in order.

2 Explain the significance of Parliament for the improvement in the lives of LGBTQ+ people in Britain in the 1950s and 1960s.

How did the fight for LGBTQ+ Rights develop in the 1970s and 1980s?

In 1967, the Sexual Offences Act legalised gay and bisexual relationships for men aged 21 and over, as long as they took place in private. It was a big step forward, but LGBTQ+ people generally continued to keep their identities and their relationships to themselves. However, this began to change in the 1970s, as some LGBTQ+ people began to fight more publicly for their rights. Yet the progress made in the 1970s didn't last: the emergence of HIV and AIDS in the 1980s saw an increase in prejudice, particularly against gay and bisexual men. What happened in the 1970s? Why did progress take a step backwards in the 1980s? And how did LGBTQ+ people fight back?

Objectives

- Describe the methods LGBTQ+ people used to fight for their rights in the 1970s.
- Discuss the impact of HIV and AIDS on the fight for LGBTQ+ Rights in the 1980s.
- Analyse how LGBTQ+ people fought back against the prejudice they experienced in the 1980s.

4.2A Out and proud in the 1970s

Britain in the 1970s

For many in Britain, the 1970s was a difficult decade. The economy was in trouble and many workers – including postal workers, waste collectors, railway workers and coal miners – went on strike. For two months in 1974, the government introduced a 'three-day week' to reduce the amount of electricity being used, because they were worried the country would run out of power.

But it was not all doom and gloom. The 1970s were also characterised by a vibrant youth culture and new music, including disco, glam rock and punk rock. Against this background, many LGBTQ+ people felt empowered to fight for their rights more publicly than they had in the 1960s.

The Gay Liberation Front

On 28 June 1969, in the USA, police raided a gay bar in New York City called the Stonewall Inn. Hundreds of LGBTQ+ people took to the streets. Protests lasted for six days, and became an iconic moment of LGBTQ+ resistance against oppression. This led to the establishment of the Gay Liberation Front in the USA. The British Gay Liberation Front (GLF) was founded in 1970 by Bob Mellors and Aubrey Walter. Within a year, nearly 300 people were attending weekly meetings, and in 1971 the group published its manifesto (a public declaration of an organisation's aims).

The GLF wanted to change society. It wanted to expose the ways in which gay people were discriminated against, and it called on gay people to make themselves visible.

▶ **SOURCE A**
The cover of the Gay Liberation Front's manifesto, published in 1971.

Connections

Another name for the Stonewall Uprising is the Stonewall Riots. Calling a protest a 'riot' makes us think of a violent public disturbance that cannot be justified. In contrast, calling a protest an 'uprising' makes us think of an act of resistance against injustice. The events in Brixton in 1981, when the Black community protested against police brutality, are also known as both the 'Brixton Riots' and the 'Brixton Uprising'.

Protest formed a key part of the GLF's strategy and they promoted the idea of protest as performance. The GLF's most famous protest was their infiltration of the Festival of Light, an event organised by religious groups concerned about the increase in sexual freedoms in society.

▼ **INTERPRETATION B** Peter Tatchell, a gay rights activist and a leading member of the GLF, recalls the Festival of Light in 1989.

'Mice were released into the audience; lesbian couples stood up and passionately embraced. A dozen GLF nuns in immaculate blue and white habits charged the platform shouting gay liberation slogans, and a GLF bishop began preaching an impromptu sermon which urged people to "keep on sinning".'

Gay Pride

On 1 July 1972, Britain's first Gay Pride march took place in London. 2,000 people participated, both celebrating LGBTQ+ identities and demanding equal rights. The organisers intentionally held the event close to the anniversary of the Stonewall Uprising.

Throughout the 1970s, the annual Pride march was an opportunity for gay people to come together and shout loudly that 'gay is fun; gay is proud; and gay is beautiful'. It was designed to challenge everyone, including the mass media and the police, who made the lives of many LGBTQ+ people very difficult.

▼ **SOURCE C** A photograph of the first Gay Pride march in 1972.

Later on...

Today, Pride events take place across the country. For example, Pride Cymru holds a weekend event in Cardiff each year. The largest Pride parade in the world is held in São Paolo, Brazil and over 4 million people attended in 2022.

Switchboard

By the end of 1974, the GLF had disbanded, but other organisations were formed to take its place.

Britain's first independent gay magazine, *Gay News*, was first published in 1972, and at its height over 18,000 copies were distributed.

The London Gay Switchboard was launched in March 1974, as a telephone helpline for LGBTQ+ people. It was initially based in a room in a London bookshop and open for just a few hours a day, but it quickly became a 24-hour service. Staffed by volunteers, it provided a wide range of support, from information about local LGBTQ+ nightlife to listening to people come out (publicly describe themselves) as LGBTQ+ for the first time. The organisation changed its name to London Lesbian and Gay Switchboard in 1986, and to Switchboard LGBTQ+ Helpline in 2015; it still operates today.

Over to You

1 a When was Britain's first Gay Pride march held?

   b Discuss why the first Pride march was an important moment in the fight for LGBTQ+ Rights in Britain.

2 a What did the GLF's manifesto state the group wanted to do?

   b Read **Interpretation B**. How did the GLF's Festival of Light protest fulfil the aims of its manifesto?

3 Is it fair to ask LGBTQ+ people to put themselves at risk by making themselves visible to fight for their rights, as suggested by the GLF manifesto? Consider both sides of the argument in your answer.

4.2B Setbacks in the 1980s

Improvements in the early 1980s

In the 1980s, councils in some areas of the country made efforts to support LGBTQ+ people and to ensure their services were more inclusive.

The Greater London Council led the way. It funded lesbian and gay community groups across the city and published *Changing the World: A London charter for gay and lesbian rights* in 1985. Manchester City Council formed an Equal Opportunities Committee in 1984, appointing both a Gay Men's Officer and a Lesbian Officer. Europe's first gay centre was built in Manchester with support from the council in 1985.

However, these positive developments in the fight for LGBTQ+ Rights were soon overshadowed.

HIV and AIDS

In 1981, people began dying from a mysterious new illness in the USA. At the time, nobody knew what caused it or understood how it spread, but the media started reporting the fact that 92 per cent of patients were gay and bisexual men. Soon the gay community was blamed for the spread of the illness.

The illness was soon identified as HIV and AIDS. HIV (Human Immunodeficiency Virus) is a virus that damages the body's immune system so that it cannot fight off infections. If left untreated, people who carry the HIV virus can develop AIDS (Acquired Immune Deficiency Syndrome), the name used to describe a collection of related illnesses that a person cannot fight off when they have HIV.

AIDS cannot be transmitted from person to person, but HIV is spread through contact with the blood, breast milk or sexual bodily fluids of an infected person. It cannot be spread through sweat, urine or saliva. The most common way to contract HIV in the UK is by having sex with an infected person without a condom.

Later on... TODAY

Today, HIV affects more heterosexual people than gay and bisexual men. There is currently no cure, but people who are diagnosed early and receive treatment will live near-normal lifespans.

On 29 October 1981, John Eaddie was the first recorded person to die of an AIDS-related illness in the UK. Gay and bisexual men were terrified, and discrimination against them increased. LGBTQ+ people worked hard to provide support and accurate information.

▼ **INTERPRETATION D** In a 2021 interview, Natasha Walker, Co-Chair of Switchboard LGBTQ+ Helpline, talks about the helpline's role supporting gay and bisexual men, and their friends and families, in the early 1980s.

'Switchboard was the leading source of information on the then new and unknown disease, installing a fifth phone line to deal with the upsurge of calls... Switchboard's volunteers collated and maintained a detailed manual of the latest and most up-to-date information available. They not only shared this with the many frightened callers to [the] helpline, but also with the general public, as volunteers staffed the BBC helplines to take calls after programmes about HIV and AIDS.'

▼ **INTERPRETATION E** Tim Tate, an investigative journalist and author, describes the discrimination gay and bisexual men experienced in the mid-1980s in a book written in 2017.

'In February 1985 the public attacks on gay men — driven by the fear of AIDS — increased. *The Sun* [newspaper] published a pronouncement by a Church of England vicar that "homosexuals offended the Lord" and that AIDS was the "wrath of God". Then, on 20 February, Health Minister Kenneth Clarke announces that the government was taking unprecedented power to detain [hold] patients in hospitals. Although he stopped short of specifying AIDS sufferers, it was clear that they were the target.'

By 1987, an average of two people a day were dying of AIDS in Britain. The government decided to run a public information campaign to educate everyone about the risks. Leaflets were delivered to every household in the country, and adverts were run on television and billboards. The campaign was considered a success: condom use increased and the number of people contracting sexually transmitted infections, including HIV, decreased. Many argue the campaign should have taken place sooner.

Jenny Lives with Eric and Martin

HIV and AIDS contributed to an increase in homophobia. In 1983, a Danish children's book called *Jenny lives with Eric and Martin* was translated into English and published by Gay Men's Press. The book tells the story of one weekend in the life of five-year-old Jenny, who lives with her dad Martin and his partner Eric. Despite the fact that only one copy had been made available to teachers in London, complaints were made about the book being available in school libraries. A lot of parents were outraged and protests followed.

▼ **SOURCE F** A photograph from *Jenny Lives with Eric and Martin*, written by Susanne Bösche and first published in Britain in 1983.

The 1987 general election

During the 1987 general election campaign, the Conservative Party harnessed this homophobia to attack Labour. It won the election with an overwhelming majority.

▼ **SOURCE G** An extract from a speech by Margaret Thatcher, leader of the Conservative Party, in 1987. The speech received a four-minute standing ovation from the crowd. 'Inalienable' means 'cannot be taken away'.

'Children who need to be taught to respect traditional moral values are being taught that they have an inalienable right to be gay... All of those children are being cheated of a sound start in life – yes cheated.'

Key Words   homophobia

Section 28

Riding high after their election victory, the Conservative government passed the Local Government Act in May 1988. Section 28 of the Act banned local authorities from 'promoting' homosexuality by teaching or publishing material. Nobody was ever prosecuted under Section 28, but for over a decade people working in schools felt unable to properly support students and their LGBTQ+ colleagues.

▼ **INTERPRETATION H** Professor Paul Baker is interested in language and in 2022 he wrote a book about Section 28.

'Section 28 made school life tense, frustrating and scary for LGBTQ+ teachers. On the face of it, such teachers should have had little to worry about... However, the wording of the section made interpretation difficult. What exactly did "promote homosexuality" mean? Even if being an out gay teacher was not promoting homosexuality, what if it caused pupils to start asking you questions about your life and relationships?... And what if a child comes to you and says "I think I might be gay, I'm being bullied by other kids and I feel like I have no one to talk to"... Is reassuring the child along the lines of "it's perfectly ok to be gay" promoting homosexuality?'

Over to You

1 a Write a sentence or two explaining what HIV and AIDS are.

  b Write a sentence explaining what Section 28 was.

2 Read **Interpretation E**. Why did HIV and AIDS lead to an increase in homophobia?

3 Read **Interpretation H**. Why did Section 28 make life difficult for LGBTQ+ teachers, according to Paul Baker?

4.2C The fightback

Lesbians and Gays Support the Miners

In 1984, coal miners belonging to the National Union of Mineworkers went on strike. They were protesting against government plans to close British coal mines (also known as 'pits'). The strike lasted almost a year, and during this time striking miners were not paid.

In London in 1984, Mark Ashton and Mike Jackson formed Lesbians and Gays Support the Miners (LGSM). They wanted to raise awareness of the strikes within the LGBTQ+ community, and to collect money for the striking miners. They saw connections between the way they were treated by the press and the government and the way the miners were treated. A few months later, Lesbians Against Pit Closures (LAPC) was also created.

LGSM's biggest charity event was a concert called 'Pits and Perverts' ('perverts' in reference to a slur that was used against gay and bisexual men which LGSM was reclaiming). Bronski Beat, a band who were all openly gay, headlined. It raised over £5,650 (over £175,000 in today's money).

In June 1985, hundreds of miners marched with LGSM at the head of London's Pride parade. Then, in October 1985, the Labour Party Conference voted to support lesbian and gay rights, after the National Union of Mineworkers overwhelmingly supported the proposal.

▼ **SOURCE J** An extract from the speech Dai Donovan, a Welsh miner supported by LGSM, gave at the 1984 'Pits and Perverts' concert.

'You have worn our badge, "Coal not Dole", and you know what harassment means, as we do. Now we will pin your badge on us; we will support you.'

Protests against Section 28

Section 28 of the 1988 Local Government Act banned local authorities from 'promoting' homosexuality by teaching or publishing material. Many people argued it was wrong, because it unfairly targeted LGBTQ+ teachers and removed support for vulnerable LGBTQ+ students in schools. There were many protests against it, and against homophobia in Britain more generally.

A notable protest was carried out in February 1988, three months before the Act was passed, when four women abseiled into the House of Lords shortly after a vote in support of the legislation. The night before Section 28 became law, a group of lesbian campaigners ran onto the set of the BBC Six O'Clock News shouting 'Stop Section 28!' Boy George, a famous pop star at the time, recorded 'No Clause 28', and many other prominent figures, including Ian McKellen and Helen Mirren, attended protests.

▼ **SOURCE I** A photograph of LGSM members marching in support of the miners in 1985.

Later on... 2014

The story of the LGSM and the striking miners is the focus of the 2014 film *Pride*.

▼ **INTERPRETATION K** In 2018, Booan Temple recalled her involvement in the BBC Six O'Clock News protest in 1988.

'I was engaged with a lesbian **feminist** network, but the campaign against Section 28 was not an organised campaign in the traditional sense… Lots of women came up with loads of very innovative protests, but none of it got reported… So a small group of us decided to go into the Six O'Clock News studio. By getting on the news, we would be the news.'

Several groups formed to oppose Section 28. One of these was Stonewall, which was created in May 1989 and named after the Stonewall Uprising in the USA. Stonewall continues to campaign for LGBTQ+ Rights today.

ACT UP

ACT UP (AIDS Coalition to Unleash Power) is an international group that was formed in 1987 in the USA to protest about the lack of government action on HIV and AIDS. ACT UP protests in Britain included die-ins (a form of peaceful protest where people lie on the ground as if they are dead) and throwing condoms into Strangeways prison in Manchester. Condoms, which protect against HIV, were not being provided to prisoners.

▼ **SOURCE L** An ACT UP poster from 1987. ACT UP's logo is an upwards-pointing pink triangle. It reclaims the symbol from the Nazis, who used a downwards-pointing pink triangle to identify gay people.

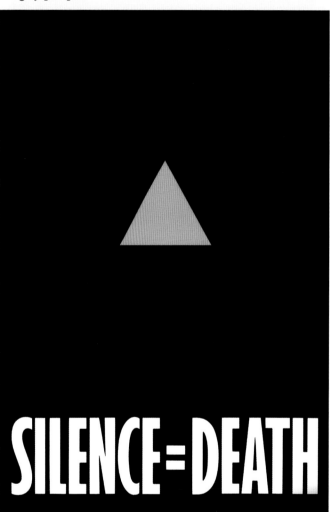

Over to You

1 a Copy and complete the table below to describe the work of LGSM and ACT UP.

Similarities	LGSM	ACT UP
What was the group's aim?		
What did the group do to achieve its aim?		

   b Write a short paragraph of no more than 75 words describing the similarities and differences between LGSM and ACT UP.

2 Suggest reasons why many striking miners in 1984–1985 and the LGBTQ+ community became allies. Use **Source J** to help you.

Knowledge and Understanding

1 Identify three facts that demonstrate progress towards equality for LGBTQ+ people in the 1970s.

2 Identify three facts that demonstrate progress took a step backwards in the 1980s.

3 'There has been steady progress towards equality for LGBTQ+ people since the beginning of the 1970s.' How far do you agree with this statement? Explain your answer.

To what extent have the lives of LGBTQ+ people improved in recent years?

During the 1980s and early 1990s, the fear surrounding HIV and AIDS led to an increase in homophobia. Section 28 of the 1988 Local Government Act also banned the 'promotion of homosexuality', making life for LGBTQ+ people, and young LGBTQ+ people in particular, increasingly difficult. However, in 1997, 18 years of Conservative government came to an end when Labour won the general election. Labour was already committed to lesbian and gay rights and, in the years that followed, the Labour government oversaw significant changes that had a positive impact on the lives of LGBTQ+ people. How did the law change? How did society become less prejudiced? And what still needs to be done?

Objectives

- Describe the laws that had a positive impact on the lives of LGBTQ+ people.
- Explain how society became less prejudiced against LGBTQ+ people.
- Recognise that the fight for LGBTQ+ Rights is ongoing.

4.3A Legal changes in the early twenty-first century

The first reforms under Labour

When Tony Blair became Prime Minister in 1997, his Labour government introduced a series of reforms.

- Following a ruling by the European Court of Human Rights, the ban on lesbian, gay and bisexual people serving in the military was lifted in January 2000.
- In 2001, the age of consent for sex between men was reduced to 16 in England, Wales and Scotland, and 17 in Northern Ireland, bringing it in line with the age of consent for sex between men and women.
- Section 28 of the 1988 Local Government Act was finally removed in Scotland in 2000 and in England and Wales in 2003.

Fact ✓

The European Convention on Human Rights protects the human rights of people living in countries signed up to the convention, including Britain. People can apply to the Court of Human Rights for a legal decision when they believe their human rights have been violated; judges in the country they live in must then take the decision into account. Human rights include the right to respect of private and family life.

▼ **SOURCE A** Carl Austin-Behan joined the Royal Air Force (RAF) in 1991; the photograph on the left shows him wearing his RAF uniform. Six years later, he was fired for being gay. In 2016, he became the first openly gay Lord Mayor of Manchester; the photograph on the right shows him wearing his ceremonial chain of office.

Gender Recognition Act

In 2004, the Gender Recognition Act was passed. For the first time, transgender people could apply to change the sex recorded on their birth certificate, from male to female or from female to male. In most cases, applicants must provide medical evidence that they have gender dysphoria (a mismatch between the biological sex they were assigned at birth and their gender identity). They must also provide evidence that they have lived in their preferred gender for at least two years, and commit to living in this gender permanently. Finally, a Gender Recognition Panel decides if the application is successful.

Landmark legislation doesn't appear from nowhere. It often comes about because people fight very hard to make it happen. Following a number of unsuccessful legal cases brought by other people, the UK was finally forced to pass the Gender Recognition Act when the European Court of Human Rights found that not being able to amend her birth certificate breached trans woman Christine Goodwin's right to privacy.

▼ **SOURCE B** In this extract from a *Huffington Post* article in 2015, Christine Goodwin's daughter talks about the impact of the case on her dad.

'She took on the might of the UK government when she realised that even though she had gone through so much to achieve "acceptance", she was still not a woman in the eyes of the law... And she won!... Now one would think that my dad lived quite happily after this... but her 15-year-long pursuit of recognition was airbrushed out of history. She was broke; the road to recognition had taken their toil physically, mentally and financially.'

Later on...

Some people argue that the Gender Recognition Act needs reforming. One of the biggest concerns is that the process people have to go through to get a gender recognition certificate is lengthy and stressful. Also, the Act only recognises two genders (male and female), which excludes people who identify in other ways, such as non-binary.

Civil partnerships

Another significant change took place in 2004, when Civil Partnership acts were passed in England, Wales, Scotland and Northern Ireland. Until this point, a relationship between two people of the same sex was not legally recognised. This could have major consequences for same-sex couples. For example, because a long-term partner was not legally recognised as a dying person's next of kin (closest living relative), they could be excluded from making decisions about their loved one's end-of-life care and funeral.

After the acts were passed, same-sex couples could register a civil partnership, which gave them virtually the same rights and responsibilities as a mixed-sex marriage, including automatically becoming their partner's next of kin. By 2013, over 66,000 civil partnerships had been registered.

Marriage (Same Sex Couples) Act

However, despite the introduction of civil partnerships, campaigners continued to argue that the legal system still discriminated against same-sex relationships: civil partnerships were a separate system and not the same as marriage. Opinion polls started showing growing support for same-sex marriages. So in 2013, the coalition government successfully passed the Marriage (Same Sex Couples) Act in England and Wales. Conservative Prime Minister David Cameron said that the legislation was one of his 'proudest moments'. A similar Act quickly followed in Scotland, and same-sex marriages became legal in Northern Ireland in 2020.

▶ **SOURCE C** A photograph of Nikki Pettit and Tania Ward, who in 2014 were the first lesbians to marry in Britain.

Over to You

1. Create a timeline showing the laws that increased rights for LGBTQ+ people in the early twenty-first century.

2. Choose one of the following laws and write a few sentences to explain why it was so significant in improving the lives of LGBTQ+ people:
   - 2004 Gender Recognition Act
   - 2013 Marriage (Same Sex Couples) Act

3. Read **Source B**. Explain why Christine Goodwin's victory at the European Court of Human Rights was bittersweet.

4.3B Social changes in the early twenty-first century

The legal changes that have done so much to improve the lives of lesbian, gay, bisexual and transgender people in Britain were made possible, in large part, by changes in social attitudes. Since the 1990s, society has generally become more accepting of LGBTQ+ people.

First kisses

In the 1990s, *EastEnders* and *Brookside* were two of the most popular long-running dramas on British television. So when the first LGBTQ+ characters were introduced to the shows, millions of viewers watched their stories, and particularly their love lives, unfold. In 1989, 17 million people watched the first gay kiss on prime-time television, between Colin and Guido, in *EastEnders*. Then five years later, six million viewers tuned in to *Brookside* to watch the first lesbian kiss between Beth and Margaret.

▼ **INTERPRETATION D** Historian Sebastian Buckle talks about the importance of gay characters in *EastEnders* in a book published in 2018.

'EastEnders was unique in providing a modern look at homosexuality through sympathetic characters seen by tens of millions of people each week.'

Gaytime TV

Gaytime TV started broadcasting on BBC2 in 1995, and ran for four years. It was the first lesbian and gay series on the BBC. Presented by comedians Rhona Cameron and Bert Tyler-Moore, it took a light-hearted look at the experiences of LGBTQ+ people in Britain. It typically featured celebrity interviews, lifestyle tips and segments on top holiday destinations for LGBTQ+ people, rather than politics and protest.

Earlier on... 1989 TO 1994

Between 1989 and 1994 Channel 4 ran a pioneering TV show called *Out on Tuesday* that focused on a wide range of LGBTQ+ stories.

▶ **SOURCE E** The tennis player Martina Navratilova was the first celebrity lesbian to be interviewed on *Gaytime TV* in June 1995.

Rainbow Laces

While LGBTQ+ people were appearing more frequently on television in the 1990s, it took longer for some sports to be more inclusive.

During the 1990s, men's football was seen as a very masculine sport, and many people involved in the game, both players and supporters, held homophobic attitudes. Justin Fashanu became the first professional footballer to publicly come out in 1990. His career suffered and it would take another 32 years before the second, Jack Daniels, did the same in 2022. At the time of writing, not one footballer in the Premier League is openly gay or bisexual.

However, football clubs have started to show their commitment to LGBTQ+ Rights by supporting the Rainbow Laces campaign. Rainbow Laces was launched by Stonewall in 2013. It encourages people taking part in sports, at professional and grassroots levels, to wear rainbow laces to make LGBTQ+ people feel welcome. And things are changing. Today, more than 50 football teams in England and Scotland have LGBTQ+ supporters clubs.

Later on... 1998

After many years as a professional footballer, Justin Fashanu retired in 1997. Tragically, a year later he died by suicide.

▶ **SOURCE F** A photograph of some of the Proud Baggies. The Proud Baggies is West Bromwich Albion's LGBTQ+ supporters club.

Across a wide range of sports, LGBTQ+ athletes are now open about their identities, including diver Tom Daley, who won gold for Britain at the 2020 Olympics, and professional boxer and fellow Olympic gold medallist Nicola Adams. Seven members of the England football team who reached the final of the FIFA Women's World Cup in 2023 are also lesbians, and many are also strong supporters of LGBTQ+ Rights.

Positive Attitude

'You should be proud of the person you are and you have nothing to be ashamed of.' It's hard not to read these words and feel encouraged by them, but they were incredibly significant for LGBTQ+ people because they were said by Prince William, the Duke of Cambridge and now Prince of Wales, in a 2017 interview with *Attitude*, a gay lifestyle magazine. If the future King is positive about LGBTQ+ people, then it signals acceptance by the majority of British society.

Raising awareness

The removal of Section 28 meant that from 2000 in Scotland and 2003 in England and Wales, schools were no longer banned from teaching about LGBTQ+ issues. One consequence of this was the setting up of LGBT History Month by Schools Out UK. It takes place every February, and is an opportunity to increase understanding and awareness of the experiences of LGBTQ+ people and to showcase many of the contributions that they have made to Britain.

Key Words

intersectionality   disability   race

Over to You

1 a What is the name of West Bromwich Albion's LGBTQ+ supporters club?

   b Why do you think many football teams now have LGBTQ+ supporters clubs?

2 Write a few sentences to explain why Prince William's interview in *Attitude* was a significant event for LGBTQ+ people.

3 Read **Interpretation D**. Why was *EastEnders* so important in changing attitudes towards LGBTQ+ people?

Connections

The term intersectionality was first used by Professor Kimberlé Crenshaw in the 1980s to describe how individual characteristics – like sex, disability, race and sexual orientation – connect with each other. It helps explain how different people experience something like homophobia differently: how a Black disabled lesbian will experience homophobia differently from a white non-disabled lesbian, for example. Organisations like UK Black Pride, Gaysians and ParaPride were established to give more LGBTQ+ people an opportunity to express their unique experiences.

▼ **SOURCE G** A photograph from a 2013 London Pride march. UK Black Pride is Europe's largest event for LGBTQ+ people of African, Asian, Caribbean, Middle Eastern and Latin American descent.

4.3C The fight for LGBTQ+ Rights is not yet over

Since the late 1990s, changing laws and social attitudes towards LGBTQ+ people have had a positive impact. LGBTQ+ people now have more rights and greater equality. However, progress isn't smooth and LGBTQ+ people continue to face a range of challenges.

Hate crime

In 1999, the Admiral Duncan pub was nearly destroyed by a nail bomb planted by someone with very strong homophobic and racist beliefs. The Admiral Duncan is a well-known gay pub in Soho, an area of central London that has been seen as a safe space for LGBTQ+ people for many years. Three people were killed and over 75 were injured.

▼ **SOURCE H** A photograph of the Admiral Duncan pub after it was bombed in 1999.

As LGBTQ+ people have become more visible, the number of hate crimes motivated by homophobia and transphobia have increased. In a 2021 survey, 64 per cent of LGBTQ+ people had experienced anti-LGBTQ+ violence and abuse. The number of hate crimes recorded by police increased from 10,817 in 2019 to 14,670 in 2021.

▼ **SOURCE I** In 2019, Chris Hannigan and Melania Geymonat, a lesbian couple, were badly beaten on a bus in a homophobic attack. In this adapted extract of a BBC interview, Chris Hannigan responds to the interviewer asking her if the attack had left her less willing to hold hands in public.

'I am not scared about being visibly queer. If anything, you should hold hands more. But I am still angry. It was scary, but this is not an unusual situation.'

Education, employment and healthcare

Although the 2010 Equality Act made it illegal to discriminate against people because of their sexual orientation or their gender reassignment, LGBTQ+ people still face many challenges in their everyday lives.

Despite the efforts some schools have made to be more inclusive, LGBTQ+ students often experience bullying. In the workplace, many LGBTQ+ people often have to hide their identities, and in some cases have had their identities revealed without their permission. Furthermore, transgender men and women have reported experiencing negative interactions with healthcare professionals because of their gender identity. There is also inequality in access to IVF treatment, which helps people who are struggling to get or stay pregnant: same-sex couples have a more expensive route to treatment.

▼ **SOURCE J** An adapted statement from the *National LGBT Survey: Summary Report*, published in 2018 by the Government Equalities Office.

'People often assume I am straight, due to wearing a wedding ring and having two children. However, in the instance when they ask about my husband, I have to think hard about whether me telling them I have a wife will impact the choices they will make in relation to the company I work for.'

Pink washing

Since 1978, the rainbow flag has been an iconic symbol of the struggle for LGBTQ+ Rights. Today, many companies use the rainbow in their marketing campaigns. On the surface, this seems like a positive sign. However, many argue these companies are pink washing their brands: they are using the rainbow to signal their support for LGBTQ+ people, and thereby attract new customers, but they are not backing this up with real action to tackle the issues that LGBTQ+ people face.

Better but not yet perfect

Looking at examples of the ways in which LGBTQ+ people experience discrimination in Britain today can be frightening. However, it's important to remember that a lot has changed since the 1950s. The law no longer criminalises loving relationships, and there is more support than ever before for young LGBTQ+ people to be who they are. LGBTQ+ people can now openly celebrate their relationships, there are lots of role models to look up to, and there are many allies too. Allies are people who don't identify as LGBTQ+ but who help in the fight for LGBTQ+ Rights. However, it is also important to recognise that the fight for LGBTQ+ Rights continues.

Meanwhile... TODAY

At the time of writing, there are 67 countries with laws making sexual relationships between people of the same sex illegal. One of these countries is Qatar. Qatar hosted the World Cup in 2022, and some players and fans showed their support for LGBTQ+ people despite FIFA, football's world governing body, banning players wearing rainbow armbands.

Over to You .ıll

1 How many homophobic and transphobic hate crimes were recorded by the police in 2021?

2 Read **Source J**. How might the experience described have a negative impact on an LGBTQ+ person's life?

3 Choose three events or individuals and explain why you would include them in a display for LGBT+ History Month.

Key Words   transphobia

▼ **SOURCE K** Another statement from the *National LGBT Survey: Summary Report*, published in 2018 by the Government Equalities Office.

'I have travelled all over the world and the UK should be proud of its progress. It is one of the best places globally to be LGBT. Things are not perfect, but this is true of many areas of life and it takes time to change attitudes.'

▼ **SOURCE L** In this photograph, the German team cover their mouths to show that they were silenced by FIFA at the World Cup in 2022.

Change and Continuity

1 Look at pages 86–89 and find three examples to show how the lives of LGBTQ+ people have improved since the 1990s.

2 Look at pages 90–91 and find three examples to show that there is still more to be done to improve the lives of LGBTQ+ people.

3 'When the Marriage (Same Sex Couples) Act was passed in 2013, the fight for LGBTQ+ Rights was won.' How far do you agree? Explain your answer.

4 Have you been learning?

⟳ Quick Knowledge Quiz

Choose the correct answer from the three options:

1 Who was the first person in Britain to undergo male to female gender affirming surgery?
- **a** Roberta Cowell
- **b** Michael Dillon
- **c** Alan Turing

2 In what year was the Wolfenden Report published?
- **a** 1956   **b** 1957   **c** 1958

3 How many years after the Wolfenden Report was published was the Sexual Offences Act passed, decriminalising consensual sexual relationships between men aged 21 and over so long as they took place in private?
- **a** 10 years
- **b** 12 years
- **c** 15 years

4 Where did the Stonewall Uprising take place?
- **a** London, UK
- **b** Paris, France
- **c** New York City, USA

5 Which British campaign group was founded in 1970?
- **a** the Beaumont Society
- **b** Stonewall
- **c** the Gay Liberation Front

6 What made it illegal for local authorities to 'promote homosexuality' by teaching or publishing material in 1988?
- **a** Section 28 of the Local Government Act
- **b** Clause 30 of the Local Government Act
- **c** Bill 32 of the Local Government Act

7 Which band headlined the Lesbian and Gays Support the Miners (LGSM) fundraising concert?
- **a** Boy George
- **b** The Beatles
- **c** Bronski Beat

8 When was the Gender Recognition Act passed?
- **a** 2001   **b** 2004   **c** 2006

9 What was the first long-running drama on British television to show a same-sex kiss?
- **a** *EastEnders*
- **b** *Brookside*
- **c** *Out on Tuesday*

10 What does pink washing mean?
- **a** when companies pretend to show support for LGBTQ+ Rights but do little to demonstrate that commitment
- **b** when football teams establish LGBTQ+ supporters clubs
- **c** when companies take a lot of positive actions to promote LGBTQ+ Rights

Literary focus

Odd one out

1 There is an odd one out in each of the following groups of historical words, phrases or names. For each group, identify the odd one out and write a sentence or two to explain why it doesn't fit in with the other words, phrases or names in the group. The first one has been done for you.

a (LGSM)   Homosexual Law Reform Society   Gay Liberation Front   ACT UP

> I have chosen LGSM because it was a group set up to support striking miners and the others are groups set up to campaign for LGBTQ+ Rights.

b   bona   gelt   dolly   tab
c   die-in   abseiling   kiss-in   arson
d   1967 Sexual Offences Act   Section 28 of the 1988 Local Government Act
     2004 Gender Recognition Act   2013 Marriage (Same Sex Couples) Act

Describing change

2 We can use a variety of terms to describe change. Here are some to consider. You may be able to think of others.

Type of change:

• political   • economic   • social

Speed of change:

• rapid   • slow   • steady

Extent of change:

• complete   • partial   • lack of

Choose three events in the fight for LGBTQ+ Rights and, for each event, describe how it changed life for LGBTQ+ people in Britain. For example:

> Protestors put pressure on the government to get rid of Section 28. They argued this **political** change was needed, campaigning **steadily** over many years until Section 28 was **completely** removed in Scotland in 2000 and in England and Wales in 2003.

Developing a documentary

3 Prepare a storyboard for a documentary about the fight for LGBTQ+ Rights.

a Begin by deciding what the title of your documentary will be. Think about the story you want to tell and choose a title that sums up that story. For example, 'The fight for LGBTQ+ Rights goes backwards in the 1980s.'

b Choose two to four important events which will help you tell your story and think about how to present them in your documentary. For example, you could choose the first Gay Pride march, the appearance of HIV and AIDS, and Section 28.

c Prepare your storyboard, explaining the choices you have made for each scene.

Glossary

activist/s   a person who fights for political or social change

age of consent   the age at which somebody is legally old enough to give consent to taking part in a sexual relationship

Bill   a proposed new law

AIDS   Acquired Immune Deficiency Syndrome; a collection of related illnesses that a person cannot fight off when they have HIV

bisexual   a person who has romantic and/or sexual relationships with people of more than one gender

boycott   when you stop using a service or a product as a form of protest

Civil Rights   political, economic and social freedoms, and equality

'colour bars'   policies that meant people of African, Caribbean and Asian heritage (collectively referred to as 'coloured' at the time) were denied opportunities available to white people, including access to jobs, restaurants, leisure facilities and housing

'coloured'   a term used to describe African, Caribbean and Asian people until the late twentieth century; it is not commonly used today because it is considered offensive

decriminalised   no longer treated as illegal

demonstration/s   a form of protest involving lots of people gathering or marching for or against something

desegregated   no longer separated

disability   occurs when the way society is organised creates barriers that prevent a person with an impairment from participating fully in daily life

discrimination   the unjust treatment of people because they belong to a particular group; people experience discrimination for many reasons, including race, gender, gender identity, sexual orientation and disability

feminists   people who believe in economic, social and political equality between men and women

first-wave feminists   people who fought for women's rights in the late nineteenth and early twentieth centuries

fourth-wave feminists   people who fought for women's rights in the age of the internet

gay   a man who has romantic and/or sexual relationships with men; also a modern term for homosexual

gender dysphoria   a mismatch between the biological sex a person was assigned at birth and their gender identity

gender   often expressed as male or female; gender is largely constructed by society and is assumed from the sex assigned at birth

gender affirming surgery   operations that change a person's physical appearance to match their gender identity

heterosexual   a man who has romantic and/or sexual relationships with women; a woman who has romantic and/or sexual relationships with men

HIV   Human Immunodeficiency Virus; a virus that damages the body's immune system so that it cannot fight off infections; can lead to AIDS if not treated

homophobia   prejudice against people who are, or who are perceived to be, lesbian, gay or bisexual

homosexual   a person who has romantic and/or sexual relationships with people of the same gender; it's an outdated term and 'gay' is more generally used today

impairment/s   when a person's body or mind is different and they might need additional support

Independent Living Movement   a movement of disabled people who want the same opportunities to make choices about how they live their lives as non-disabled people have

intersectionality   a term used to describe how individual characteristics – like gender, class, race and sexual orientation – connect with each other; it helps explain how different people experience something like sexism or disablism differently

legacy   a situation that exists now because of events, actions and so on that took place in the past

lesbian   a woman who has romantic and/or sexual relationships with women

LGBTQ+   stands for Lesbian, Gay, Bisexual, Transgender, Queer or Questioning, with the + representing the wide variety of other sexual orientations and gender identities

'marriage bar'   women were expected to quit their jobs when they got married, to focus on being wives and mothers

medical model   a model of disability that focuses on impairments as conditions that are 'wrong' and in need of 'fixing'

migrants   people who have moved from one place to another to live permanently; sometimes referred to as 'immigrants' when they arrive to live permanently in a foreign country

militant   violent

misogyny   hatred of women

next of kin   closest living relative; this is usually your husband or wife

non-binary   a person whose gender identity doesn't sit comfortably with 'male' or 'female'

patriarchy   the system that gives men power and largely excludes women from power

pop culture   popular culture expressed through mass media (music, television, radio, cinema, newspapers and, today, through the internet); pop culture is generally aimed at younger people

pressure group   an organisation that tries to influence government policy and/or public opinion to achieve its aims

queer   a term used by people who do not want to use a specific label to describe who they do or do not have romantic and/or sexual relationships with, and/or do not want to use traditional terms to describe their gender identity; some LGBTQ+ people think the word is insulting, but others embrace it

race   a grouping of humans according to shared physical features, such as skin colour, hair texture and facial features; examples of different races include Black, white, Asian and South East Asian

racism   prejudice against people from a particular ethnic group, typically a minority ethnic group

refugee   someone forced to leave their home to escape war, persecution or a natural disaster

riot a violent public disorder

second-wave feminists people who fought for women's rights in the 1960s, 1970s and 1980s

segregated separated, for example by race, gender or religion

sexism prejudice on the grounds of one's sex or gender, typically against women

sexual orientation an umbrella term that describes who a person is sexually or romantically attracted to

social injustice the unequal and unfair treatment of different groups in society

social model a way of viewing disability that believes a person is disabled because of the way society is organised

stereotype a widely held but oversimplified belief about a particular group of people

strike workers get together and refuse to work, in the hope their employer will respond to their demands, e.g. for better pay

suffrage the right to vote

suffragettes campaigners for the right of women to vote, who organised often violent protests to advance their cause

suffragists campaigners for the right of women to vote, who used peaceful means of protest

third-wave feminists people who fought for women's rights in the 1990s and 2000s

trade union a group of workers doing the same or similar jobs who join together to form an organisation that will protect their rights and further their interests

transgender people whose gender is not the same as, or does not sit comfortably with, the sex they were assigned at birth

transphobia prejudice against people who are, or who are perceived to be, transgender

uprising an act of resistance

visibility being widely seen

Index